Cou~~~~~~
~ of ~
WASHINGTON

A Guide Book
from Country Roads Press

Country Roads
~ of ~
WASHINGTON

Archie Satterfield

Illustrated by
Kathy Bray

Country Roads Press
CASTINE · MAINE

Country Roads of Washington
© 1993 by Archie Satterfield. All rights reserved.

Published by Country Roads Press
P.O. Box 286, Lower Main Street
Castine, Maine 04421

Text and cover design by Edith Allard
Illustrations by Kathy Bray
Cover by Victoria Sheridan

ISBN 1-56626-034-5

Library of Congress Cataloging-in-Publication Data
Satterfield, Archie.
    Country roads of Washington / by Archie Satterfield ;
illustrated by Kathy Bray
        p. cm.
    Includes bibliographical references and index.
    ISBN 1-56626-034-5 : $9.95
        1. Automobile travel—Washington (State)—
Guidebooks. 2. Washington (State)—Guidebooks.
3. Rural roads—Washington (State)   I. Title.
GV1024.S317   1993
917.97'04—dc20   93-24892
                                                      CIP

Printed in the United States of America.
10 9 8 7 6 5 4 3 2 1

To By Fish, who taught me
that humor doesn't have to hurt

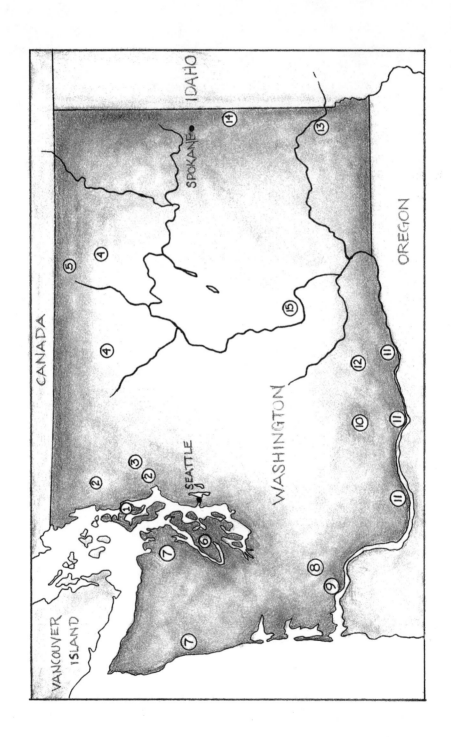

Contents

(& Key to Washington Country Roads)

	Introduction	ix
1	Slow Road to Bellingham	1
2	State 9 to Canada	8
3	Mountain Loop Highway	14
4	From Puget Sound to the Pend Oreille	19
5	An Okanogan Loop	30
6	Inside Hood Canal	35
7	US 101	40
8	Through the Heart of Lewis County	52
9	Down the Columbia to the Sea	59
10	A Gifford Pinchot Excursion	65
11	The Columbia Gorge Route	72
12	Bickleton: Bluebirds in Horse Heaven	80
13	The Snake River Canyon	84
14	The Best of the Palouse	89
15	Crab Creek Valley	95
16	Moses Coulee	101
	Bibliography	105
	Index	107

Introduction

While working on this book I was at a dinner party in Bellingham and the guests, most of whom were from elsewhere, were talking about how they arrived in Washington. Most of us had a similar experience: From the moment we arrived in the state it was love at first sight.

In my case, I had been to Washington three summers working on wheat farms while attending university in Missouri. I love Washington's wheat country, and it was the wonderful people there that convinced me I should come to Washington to stay. I wasn't prepared for the effect the Puget Sound area would have on me the first time I saw it. This occurred late one September afternoon when I came down from Snoqualmie Pass over the Mercer Island floating bridge into Seattle. I was already committed to staying in Washington, but growing to love the state had been a gradual process while I drove tractors and combines in the Washtucna area.

When I saw Puget Sound for the first time, it was almost like the first time I saw that girl wearing a deerskin jacket at a dance in Buena Vista, Colorado. I was only sixteen then and couldn't tell the difference between galloping hormones and good judgment. I was twenty-six when I arrived in Seattle and knew the difference, more or less. This experience was an epiphany, not a glandular reaction.

Immediately after arriving in eastern Washington to work on Chet and Pearl Bell's farm about halfway between Ritzville and Washtucna, I began traveling around that area as a willing passenger with Chet in the pickup and, when Pearl wasn't using it, in the family car. We went to Kahlotus and we went to Lind, Lacrosse, Benge, occasionally to Spokane, over to Colfax, and several times a week to Washtucna and Ritzville. We went to virtually every farm within a radius of fifty miles because Chet, who died in 1980, was perhaps the most sociable person I have ever known. In the process I became intimately acquainted with that part of Washington and I especially liked the wide diversity within a region that at first glance looks much the same. I learned where the Old Mullan Road ran along part of the Palouse River, and I saw the Little Falls of the Palouse, the channeled scablands, the Palouse Hills, the Big Bend area, several coulees, sudden little lakes appearing in the dry country, and so forth.

Once when it rained and Chet couldn't think of anything better to do, he took me somewhere west of Washtucna to show me the shortest windmill in the world. I thought he was playing a practical joke on me but there it was: a windmill that sat right on the ground, barely tall enough for its blades to clear the plowed ground around it. Chet said that the wind blew the same speed on the ground as thirty feet in the air, so why build a tower?

Since those wonderful summers, when Chet paid me even though I often did nothing more than lean against the pickup fender while he joked with his friends, I have been addicted to traveling around Washington. I managed to travel some while I worked on the *Longview Daily News*, mostly along the Lower Columbia River. When I went to work on the Seattle newspapers I worked in much more travel, talking photographers into going with me all over the state. I always lived in fear that the management would decide I wasn't making the trips worthwhile, so I tried always to come back to the office with at least one additional story. Admittedly, some of them were pretty thin, but my trips continued.

I've never been bored traveling in the state, although I-5 between Olympia and Longview does get awfully long after a trip through the southern part of the state. I console myself by remembering how long it is across southern Wyoming on I-80. We have so much diversity in Washington that we are prone to take it for granted until we visit other parts of the country with less.

To simplify road designations, I've used the following abbreviations: I=Interstate, US=U.S. Route or Highway, State=State Route or Highway.

The fifteen routes selected here are among my favorites. I could have included as many more, mostly shorter routes I've taken over the years, but I think the limitations imposed by the publisher have been beneficial because they forced me to select those I think are the very best. I hope you will agree.

Country Roads
~ of ~
WASHINGTON

A Guide Book
from Country Roads Press

1 ~

Slow Road to Bellingham

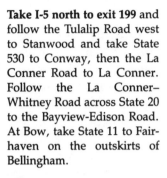

Take **I-5 north to exit 199** and follow the Tulalip Road west to Stanwood and take State 530 to Conway, then the La Conner Road to La Conner. Follow the La Conner–Whitney Road across State 20 to the Bayview-Edison Road. At Bow, take State 11 to Fairhaven on the outskirts of Bellingham.

Highlights: *Beaches, sloughs, parks, dairy farms, small towns, tulip and daffodil fields, tourist towns, rugged coastline, country inns and restaurants.*

I've probably made more than 100 trips to Vancouver over the past decade to spend weekends with friends, to attend dinner parties, or simply to give my car some exercise. It is exactly 120 miles from my home to a friend's houseboat in Vancouver's Coal Harbour, and most of those miles are through pretty scenery on I-5. But even the Grand Tetons would become overly familiar if you saw them from the same vantage point day after day, so I have found various routes and variations thereof to spice up my visits to Vancouver.

This route is one of my favorites because it follows the shoreline of Puget Sound as closely as highway engineers and geography permit and it adds only about an hour to the trip and perhaps thirty additional miles.

Driving north from Seattle on I-5, begin this trip at exit 199, marked Marysville-Tulalip, and go west beneath the interstate into the Tulalip Indian Reservation. (By the way, it is pronounced two-*lay*-lip, not *two*-la-lip, as I pronounced it on arrival in Washington.) The road generally follows the shoreline, which features a few sloughs where fishing boats and tugs are parked picturesquely. Clusters of expensive waterfront homes line some of the bluffs and bays, most of which were built on reservation land that was leased from the Tulalip tribe. In case you're a gambler, the Tulalip were one of the first tribes in Washington to establish gambling casinos to increase tribal income.

Beach access is limited on the reservation, but the marine and forest scenery is pretty and you'll find an occasional convenience store. Be patient; shortly after leaving the reservation you will come to Kayak Point County Park, which is one of Puget Sound's nicest county-owned parks. The point juts out into the sound at the base of a steep bluff. The 670-acre park has broad lawns for sports, a good clamming beach, picnic tables, a shelter that can be reserved for a fee, campsites, and a boat launching area.

From Kayak Point the road ambles through second-growth timber and between suburban homes and quickly goes through Warm Beach, a small community that got its name from the shallow bay where the sun warms the salt water enough for comfortable wading and swimming. Soon the road swings back inland against the bluffs with enough elevation to avoid being inundated at low tide. To the west the land is flat and protected from flooding by dikes and occasional drainage ditches to keep brackish water from covering crops and grazing land. As with nearly all flatland between Seattle and the Canadian border, fat Holsteins with udders almost dragging on the ground graze between milking times. This is some of the best dairy farming land in America and the major dairy cooperative, Darigold, exports thousands of tons more dairy products than it can sell in the Northwest.

Stanwood is the first town of significance after you leave Marysville. It is primarily a farming town with some allowances for tourism and the growing population on Camano Island just west of town. As islands go, Camano isn't much because it is separated from the mainland only by a saltwater ditch spanned by a short bridge. Nearly all of the island has been turned into building lots, and it is a popular second-home and retirement community.

The main route, which now is State 530, continues north from Stanwood across the broad, flat landscape created by the estuary of the Skagit River. Over the centuries the river has swung back and forth over several miles, dumping its load of silt to create some of the richest farming land in the Northwest. The estuary is composed of several branches of the river that have been diked to prevent nearly annual flooding. The efforts are only marginally successful, and in spite of the prospect of having everything soaked, if not washed away, people have insisted on building their homes on this land that is as flat as an airport runway with an elevation of only inches above sea level. Thus, almost every winter the newspapers and television stations send crews to the Skagit valley to report on the latest disaster, which could easily have been prevented by working the land but living on high ground elsewhere.

Route 530 bumps into I-5 at Conway, but this trip takes a sharp left at Conway and continues across the farmland toward La Conner. Conway is a very small town with a large and slightly rickety old wooden building that serves as a farmers' market during the long growing season. Three and some-

3

times four crops are grown on the land here, thanks to the moderate climate and rich soil.

From Conway onward is the most popular part of this trip because the farms here grow bulbs—tulips, daffodils, and iris—thousands of acres of them, and when they are blooming in the spring the roads are clogged with cars, tour buses, bicycles, joggers, and volksport walking clubs. It is one of the Northwest's most beautiful sights and film manufacturers' local sales figures rise dramatically during this period.

The road between Conway and La Conner is a typical farm road; its route is dictated by property lines and local geography, so be prepared for corners rather than curves as it goes between farms and across ditches and arms of the Skagit River delta. At one point it gains perhaps 200 feet in elevation along Pleasant Ridge and gives a great view of the fields with Mount Vernon off in the middle distance and the Cascade Range forming the horizon. Several beautiful homes line the ridge, including at least one bed and breakfast in a Victorian home.

La Conner is one of those tiny towns that began its life as a fishing and farming village, but grew into something quite different. It is near the southern end of Swinomish Channel, a shallow and generally narrow saltwater channel that separates Fidalgo Island from the mainland. Like the people of Camano Island, very few residents of Fidalgo consider it a true island, although legally speaking it is.

La Conner was discovered many years ago by Seattle-area artists, led by Guy Anderson. They liked the isolation, the casual and inexpensive life-style, and the scenery that inspired some of their best artwork. They painted the flat farmland with mountain backdrops, the fishing boats, and the fog that often hangs on the land and turns the few trees into spectral visions. The novelist Tom Robbins moved there long before he became famous and a cult figure, and some of

The waterfront at La Conner

his novels and his essays for *Esquire* magazine described the area vividly.

Today La Conner is one of the most popular destinations for Washington visitors. I go there often because most of my out-of-town visitors have heard of it and women like it because it has so many shops. When I am traveling alone, I seldom bother getting out of the car unless I am going into the Valley Museum of Northwest Art in the Gaches Mansion, where the work of regional artists is on display and quality exhibits are hung.

However, each spring I do go to the various farms that sell tulips. My favorite is West Shore Acres just north of La Conner along Swinomish Channel. The old-fashioned farmhouse is surrounded by thousands of tulips of every color and size, and the three or four photos I intend to take always grow into a roll or more. And I always relent and have freshly cut tulips shipped to someone.

5

From La Conner this route heads due north on the La Conner–Whitney Road across State 20 and on to Bayview, where a state park overlooks the tideflats of Padilla Bay, the enormous petroleum refinery at March Point, Anacortes, Guemes Island, and the other San Juan Islands. The park is beautiful and I am partial to it because one of my daughters was married there in an outdoor ceremony. Shortly after leaving Bayview, the road ducks inland over a hill and through tall timber, then emerges with views north across the small Samish River and Samish Bay to Chuckanut Mountain.

The road ends at a T-intersection where a left turn will take you out to Samish Island, another island barely separated by a ditch. It is a small, slender island almost completely covered with homes. The right turn puts you on the main route to the small town of Edison, where you can stop for a snack and conversation in one of two taverns.

About a mile farther is State 11, the famous Chuckanut Drive. Turn left, or north, at this intersection. Here you will find a good restaurant, the Rhododendron Cafe, as well as a couple of stores that stock antiques and general "stuff." A farm nearby has posted two signs beside the road: "Drive Quietly" and "Meadow Larks Singing." The route runs across more flatland until it reaches the shoreline at the foot of Chuckanut Mountain. Here the road crosses a bridge and suddenly you are following the edge of the mountain above the shallow water that turns into tideflats at low tide. A clear-cut patch on the very top of Chuckanut Mountain has turned it into a popular launching pad for hang gliders, who soar out over the tideflats and come back to the flat fields below to land.

Chuckanut Drive was Washington's first highway built for scenery alone. It clings to the face of the mountains something like a shortened version of California's State 1. Because the mountains along here are so steep few homes have been built, but the Burlington Northern railroad ran tracks along the base of the mountain, and within a few years passenger service is expected to be available again between Vancouver and Seattle. In spite of the steep mountainside, three restaurants have been in business there many years, one almost at the southern end of the drive and the other two a few miles farther north, both of which cling to the steep cliff like swallows' nests.

Three bed and breakfasts are at the very southern end of the drive. One is owned by Oyster Creek Inn, and another is upstairs in Chuckanut Manor Restaurant. Another place worth a stop is the oyster farm just below Oyster Creek Inn. Visiting hours are posted on the gate behind the inn.

Toward the end of the drive is Larrabee State Park with good picnic areas and overnight camping.

The roadway is extremely crooked and is subject to washouts and slides during the winter. Wherever possible, the state has added turnouts so you can enjoy the views across to Lummi Island and the San Juan Islands. During the summer months portable toilets are placed at some of the turnouts.

Chuckanut Drive ends almost suddenly in Fairhaven, a Victorian village that is part of Bellingham, and the decidedly mundane I-5 is only a short distance away.

In the Area

All phone numbers are in area code 206.

Gaches Mansion, 466-4288

La Conner Chamber of Commerce, 466-4778

Chuckanut Manor Restaurant and Bed and Breakfast, 766-6191

Oyster Creek Inn, 766-6179

Larrabee State Park, 676-2093

2 ~

State 9 to Canada

Take State 9 from Woodinville straight north to the Canadian border at Sumas.

Highlights: *One of the last coast-to-coast highways, U.S.– Canadian border, rich farmland, meandering country roads, peaceful views, small villages; North Cascades National Park, Mount Baker.*

This route is a slower but pretty alternate to I-5 that takes you past farms and lakes to the edge of the Cascade Range. It goes through well-tended small towns and is never more than five miles from any of the major towns—Everett, Marysville, Mount Vernon, and Bellingham—along the route. It also makes a good alternate route to and from British Columbia.

Washington shunpikers love State 9 because it parallels I-5 from the Seattle area almost all the way to the Canadian border, but offers a flavor of times past when people went "motoring." State 9 is one of those routes taken by people who still drive for pleasure.

It has the advantage of being close to the main north-south arterial of I-5, and you can drive the whole length or only certain segments that appeal to you. For example, at Snohomish the highway crosses US 2, one of the last coast-to-coast highways. It crosses State 92 at Lake Stevens, and State 530 at Arlington, which are each end of the Mountain Loop Highway. It also crosses State 20, the North Cascades Highway, and State 542, the Mount Baker Highway. Each of these highways takes you to nearby towns that are larger than those on State 9, and they take you to I-5 if you've had your fill of pastoral scenes.

The route begins at Woodinville and bisects the suburbia that keeps sprawling farther and farther north. You won't miss much if you don't bother taking State 9 until you reach Arlington. From Arlington north it is a more honest country road. The road is more crooked and narrow, has less traffic, and you get to see bucolic scenery and smell bucolic smells. Rather than cutting straight across the good farmland, it winds along the edge of hillsides overlooking the valleys, and sometimes it climbs over a low hill to the next valley.

After leaving Arlington, the route will take you through some heavy timber, past a few privately owned tree farms, and around sharp curves. You will reach Lake McMurray, which is mostly a residential area with summer cabins sprinkled among the more substantial homes. The next town is Clear Lake, a small village with false-front store buildings and a Quonset hut that probably dates back to the end of World War II, when these buildings were sold off as surplus.

You'll also note that many houses along here stand almost against the highway blacktop. The owners didn't build that close to the highway by choice. At one time the homes had real yards and were several feet back, but as the highway was widened, the front yards were gobbled up by the blacktop and the right of way.

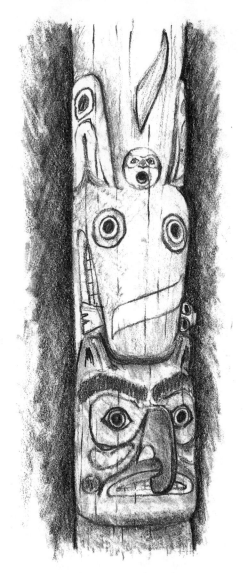

En route to Canada

The highway continues on past Mount Vernon, missing it by only a mile or two, then goes through Sedro Woolley and crosses State 20, the North Cascades Highway. Sedro Woolley came by its unusual name in a typically mixed-up bureaucratic fashion. It was named *Cedro*, Spanish for "cedar," by locals because so much cedar grew in the area. The Post Office Department accepted the name, but with its spelling of Sedro. A man named Woolley built his own town nearby and you know what happened when the two merged.

Sedro Woolley contains the headquarters of the North Cascades National Park and it has several gift shops and art galleries.

For the remainder of the trip to the Canadian border the landscape alternates between flatland used for dairy farming and berry growing, and trees. You'll see several nurseries along the way that grow Alberta spruce, which grows into a perfect cone shape. All Alberta spruce we see now are the offspring of a single "sport" from a tree found in the Canadian province of Alberta. The oddly shaped branch found growing on that tree was cut off and propagated, thus creating a whole new species of ornamental tree.

The first hills of the Cascade Range loom almost overhead from time to time and on clear days 10,778-foot Mount Baker will suddenly appear through the trees or between the hills. Before Mount St. Helens became active again in 1980, seismic activity began on Mount Baker and people assumed that if any of the Cascade volcanoes would erupt, it would be Mount Baker. However, Mount Baker cooled down and Mount St. Helens took over in a big way.

Wickersham, Acme, Van Zandt, Deming, and Lawrence still exist but their commercial thunder has been stolen by the larger towns on I-5 that State 9 avoids. Everson and Nooksack are a bit larger, and Sumas, on the U.S.–Canadian border, is the largest town on the route after Sedro Woolley. Sumas, however, is mostly a border town, a place for Canadians to come across to buy cheaper gasoline and to shop. Many Canadians who do business in the United States rent post office boxes in border towns to avoid the delays caused when mail must cross back and forth across the international border.

Few countries in the world are better neighbors than the United States and Canada. The United States has continually irked Canada for various reasons, paramount among which is that the United States has simply ignored Canada because it is so peaceful. The boundary between the two countries is one of the longest in the world—from the Arctic Ocean down to Washington, then all the way across the continent to Maine and New Brunswick. This boundary is not patrolled on a regular basis, nor does it have guard towers, barbed-wire fences, or searchlights. It is supposedly the longest border in the world without these unfortunate markers.

For a look at this situation, take Halverstick Road west just outside Sumas and follow it to Northwood Road, then turn right (north) on it and go to Boundary Road, which soon turns left (west). Boundary Road is a two-lane blacktop road featuring farmhouses and barns on the south side, and a ditch on the north with utility poles planted in the ditch. Across the ditch is another two-lane blacktop road with houses and barns facing south. It took me a moment to figure out this mirror image when I first saw it, but then I saw a mailbox adorned with the Canadian maple leaf and that explained it: The ditch is the international boundary.

In theory, you are subject to a substantial fine if you walk across the ditch into Canada without clearing customs. But in practice the authorities do not interfere with the friendships that normally develop between the neighbors. One benefit of this tolerance policy is that the farmers on both sides keep an eye on the border and report anything suspicious they happen to see.

In the Area

All phone numbers are in area code 206.

Skagit Valley Visitor Information Center, 757-4514
Bellingham/Whatcom Visitors Bureau, 671-3990

3 ~

Mountain Loop Highway

From Everett: Take US 2 to State 9, go north to Lake Stevens junction with State 92 to Granite Falls. In Granite Falls, follow the Mountain Loop Highway signs to Darrington.

Highlights: *Granite Falls on the South Fork Stillaguamish River and Granite Falls Fishway; numerous picnic areas and campgrounds, trails for short hikes, secluded lakes, ice caves, bald eagles in the winter, the boulder-filled Sauk River.*

This fifty-five-mile loop trip seems designed for Sunday drives, and from June through October few places in the Puget Sound basin are more popular. Fortunately the area boasts so many picnic areas, trailheads, campgrounds, and one- or two-car-size turnouts that it can absorb a lot of people before it starts feeling crowded.

This is one of the first drives I took into the heart of the Cascades shortly after my arrival, and any doubts I may have had about my choice of a new home were dispelled by the trip. My love for this route even survived two bad experiences on it. One was my first actual camping trip. I had camped out while working during wheat harvest and on cattle ranches but never for fun, and my first such experience was on the shore of Bear Lake, with people who not only couldn't tolerate solitude, but also didn't think highly of people who wanted to be alone for a few minutes. The only way I could get my necessary alone time was to paddle out into the middle of the lake on a poorly constructed raft that would support only one person and sit there pouting while pretending I was fishing for eastern brook trout.

The next episode occurred just after my first child was born. The car broke down—that particular 1954 Plymouth broke down often and always in out-of-the-way places. While I was looking at the engine, the seat of my pants ripped out. Almost at the same moment, our infant daughter gave a kick worthy of Pelé and my wife spilled a chocolate milk shake on her white shorts. I wrapped a sweater around my waist to cover my white underpants flashing in the sun and she draped the baby's blanket over her stained shorts. Thus clad, we traipsed back to a store and tried to look calm and collected while we waited for a friend to bring us a fuel pump.

The first several miles of the drive between Everett and Granite Falls are rather disappointing because the route runs through the urban sprawl that is slowly eating away at the Cascade foothills. Once you reach Granite Falls, the land becomes Mount Baker–Snoqualmie National Forest and the clusters of new homes are left behind.

Just outside the town of Granite Falls you will cross the high bridge over the South Fork Stillaguamish River. Stop here for a walk beside the falls and along the Granite Falls Fishway, which was built many years ago to enable salmon to migrate past the falls. At one time this fish ladder was the longest in the world, but that claim now belongs to another somewhere else in the world.

The paved highway continues on, following the course of the North Fork of the Stillaguamish River, locally known as the Stilly, and fishermen are always out in season, working the riffles and pools in search of rainbow, eastern brook, and steelhead. Every turn gives you a new and equally beautiful view of the river, its steep valley, and the forested mountains on either side. Numerous trails lead off the main road to viewpoints or small lakes tucked away above the valley.

This first portion of the loop along the Stillaguamish came into being after a substantial gold and silver discovery was made back in the Cascades in 1889. The discovery was named Monte Cristo, and it was so promising that a railroad was built from Puget Sound to the mine. All of this activity caught the attention of prominent East Coast investors, in-

If you're lucky, you may see elk browsing

cluding the Rockefeller family, and as a result the town of Everett grew at the west end of the Monte Cristo railroad. Then the Great Northern Railroad came through Everett and its future was secure, even though the crash of 1893 and the recession that lasted until 1897 dealt it a hard blow. The Monte Cristo mine created a lot of jobs in the area and the town of Monte Cristo grew up around it and Silverton, down the river a few miles. As with all mines, ore is finite and eventually the gold and silver ran out, quickly turning Monte Cristo into an almost-ghost-town and relegating Silverton to a minor role in the scheme of things.

Only a short distance from the Bear Lake turnoff you'll find the Red Bridge Forest Service campground. Nearby is an old mining tunnel that goes back into the mountain about 125 feet, and along the river are remnants of the railroad that ran from Everett to Monte Cristo.

Just down the road from Silverton is the site of a resort complex named the Big Four Inn in honor of the mountain of the same name that stands in the background. The inn burned in 1949 and was never rebuilt. Instead, a forest service campground was built on the site, and a mile-long trail leads across the river on a bridge and into the mountains to the so-called ice caves. The caves aren't really ice but packed snow. They are created by water running beneath the snowpack. They can be treacherous; not long ago one of the caves collapsed on some people. Check with the Verlot Ranger Station for information and conditions on your way in.

Because the Monte Cristo townsite is privately owned, your chances of seeing it are slim, unless the owner decides to open it again. From the Monte Cristo turnoff, the Mountain Loop Highway takes a sharp left turn to the north and is gravel the rest of the way to Darrington. The road soon joins the Sauk River and follows its course north. Numerous campgrounds have been built along this route, and you'll have several choices of trails to hike back into the national forest and the Henry M. Jackson Wilderness. Glacier Peak isn't far from the Sauk River, and you can hike out of the river valley for good views of the peak if you don't want to hike all the way to it.

Fishing is good in the Sauk River, and the rapids are popular with white water enthusiasts.

The road eventually arrives in Darrington, which is one of the more interesting towns along the base of the Cascade Range. Like so many towns in the foothills, it began as a logging town and most of its original residents were from the Carolinas, self-proclaimed Tar Heels and very proud of it. They brought with them their strong family traditions, social customs, and their bluegrass and country music. Each July the town hosts a bluegrass festival that brings tourists and musicologists from all over the West.

At Darrington you have a choice of continuing north on paved State 530 to Rockport on State 20, the North Cascades Highway, or you can turn back west on State 530 to Arlington and back to I-5. The road to Rockport winds through forests and past streams and lakes, while the route to Arlington takes you through a more populated area, past several farms and campgrounds.

In the Area

All phone numbers are in area code 206.

Verlot Ranger Station, 691-7791

Darrington Ranger Station, 436-1155

Darrington Chamber of Commerce, 436-0223

4 ~

From Puget Sound to the Pend Oreille

From Port Townsend take State 20 east.

Highlights: *Victorian town of Port Townsend, ferry ride to Whidbey Island and Deception Pass; the Skagit valley, North Cascades National Park, Okanogan Highlands, and the Pend Oreille River valley.*

Almost any time you see a list of the prettiest country roads in America, State 20 will be mentioned. Other highways may be more spectacular in places, but I don't know of any with so much variety of beautiful scenery.

This trip crosses almost the entire state, from the western side of Puget Sound to Idaho. It is described in a west-to-east direction.

State 20 leaves US 101 at the south end of Discovery Bay on the Olympic Peninsula and heads north to Port Townsend, that most Victorian of Washington towns. Port Townsend began with very high hopes. Its citizenry was convinced it would become the San Francisco of the Northwest, and indeed, it was the port of entry for all foreign vessels and several governments had their consulates in mansions along the top of the steep bluff overlooking the town and the entrance to Puget Sound. Unfortunately, the town's future fizzled when the railroad stopped its westward movement dead in its tracks in Seattle and Tacoma, leaving Port Town-

The Hastings House in Port Townsend

send an isolated appendage. It would be nearly a century before the town came into its own as a trendy place for Seattleites and Californians to escape the urban rat race for what they hoped would be a small-town atmosphere.

Fort Worden, one of the three army posts built to protect the entrance of Puget Sound, was built on the edge of town, and it was eventually abandoned and turned over to the state parks system. This, too, has been a boon to Port Townsend because it was turned into a performing arts center with frequent concerts, and an enormous Quonset hut became a foundry for sculptors.

From Port Townsend, State 20 hitches a ride on a Washington State Ferry across Admiralty Inlet, which is the entrance to Puget Sound, and crosses Keystone on Whidbey Island. This is one of the more interesting of the Washington ferry rides because all ship traffic to and from Puget Sound is funnelled through the narrow inlet and sometimes the large ships seem to be staging a parade as they steam through. Also, the tides flow rapidly through the inlet, almost like a swift river, and when the tides are unusually low some of the ferry schedules are suspended because the Keystone landing area on Whidbey Island is too shallow.

The Keystone landing is at the foot of the hill on which Fort Casey State Park sits. The fort, one of the three original guardians of Puget Sound, was the recipient of the last intact ten-inch "disappearing rifles." Actually cannons, these odd weapons were used for harbor defense between the world wars. When the cannons were fired, the recoil caused them to swing backwards and down out of sight so they could be reloaded in safety. The sighter stayed aboard the cannon for the whole procedure, getting a wild ride and sometimes a perfect black eye caused by the recoil, which drove the sighting scope into his face. These cannon were originally teamed with a set of enormous mortars, but the mortars were removed shortly after the first test firing; the concussion broke windows for miles around and gave children night-mares for weeks. It was much like riding out frequent Mount St. Helens eruptions. The cannon at Fort Casey were removed from a military base in the Philippines and given to the fort. They obviously don't work anymore, but a walk around them will give you an idea of how Rube Goldberg could have been credited with inventing them.

State 20 heads north up Whidbey Island, the longest island in the lower forty-eight states, past the false-front town of Coupeville and through Oak Harbor before leaving the island at Deception Pass State Park. This is the state's most popular park, and you will understand why when you cross the Deception Pass Bridge. The salt water at the bottom of the chasm below the bridge is in almost constant motion as the tide rushes back and forth through it, creating whirlpools and backwashes.

After crossing Deception Pass, the route swings east and you are soon in the Skagit valley, some of the Northwest's most productive farmland. Among the crops are tulip, iris, and daffodil bulbs, and each spring the valley floor is com-posed of bands of solid color as the flowers bloom. Several farms sell tulips retail and will ship them anywhere in the world.

Soon after crossing I-5 you will go through Sedro Wool-ley, a mostly agricultural town where the headquarters for North Cascades National Park are located beside the highway on the eastern edge of town. Here you can stock up on maps, brochures, and other information on traveling through the Cascades.

The foothills of the Cascades appear almost immediately after you leave Sedro Woolley. The highway follows the Skagit River upstream for several miles. One of the state's most popular rivers, steelhead fishermen love to drift it with guides, and naturalists love it because bald eagles migrate down from Canada and Alaska by the dozen and congregate each fall to feast on salmon.

Just before entering the Cascades, you will go through the town of Concrete, so named because it was built around a factory that made cement. When the factory closed, most citizens expected the town to fade into oblivion, but it has thrived as a recreational and retirement town, and most recently film studios have discovered it as a place to shoot stories set in the 1950s because its downtown buildings have hardly changed since that period.

After Concrete you are in the Cascades and the climb begins. The highway still follows the Skagit, but for most of the year it is hardly more than a shadow of its former self because of the hydroelectric dams built decades ago to supply Seattle with electricity. Sometimes the river is virtually dry, then suddenly a wall of water will come rushing down it as the dam floodgates are opened. Some of the most popular tours in the Cascades are the Seattle City Light Skagit Tours, which take much of the day. The cost of a full tour includes a family-style meal after you've toured the dams and power plants and gone for a ride on the Incline Railway lift.

The highway bisects the North Cascades National Park, and the area on both sides of the highway has been designated a National Recreational Area so that some support services, not permitted within national parks, can be available. The park service also maintains a cluster of campgrounds in the area. But be warned; you can't buy gasoline for almost seventy-five miles after leaving Marblemount, so check your fuel gauge. The highway isn't particularly easy to drive at night, either. Because it is cleared of snow so often, the center line and edge markers are scraped off by snowplows and the paint is hardly visible. During a rainstorm or on a foggy night you must drive at almost a crawl.

The highway is closed between Marblemount and Mazama during the winter by snow and the danger of avalanches. It usually closes by Christmas and opens in May or June, depending on the amount of snow and avalanche danger.

You will go over two passes on the way across—4,855-foot Rainy Pass and 5,477-foot Washington Pass. Just beyond Washington Pass is a turnout above the crooked highway with a view across the jagged peaks. It is one of the best views in the Cascade Range.

From Washington Pass the highway runs downhill for several miles through open pine forests to the Methow valley and its western towns of Mazama and Winthrop. Mazama isn't much for size but it has some of the nicest family resorts in the area, specializing in outdoor recreation such as cross-country skiing and backpacking.

If you have an extra hour or two, you may want to take a side trip from Mazama over 6,797-foot Harts Pass, to Slate Peak, the highest point in Washington to which you can drive the family car. The peak is 7,440 feet high, and the dirt road to it is kept in good condition because it is used by both sightseers and hikers on the Pacific Crest Trail, which crosses the road just below the peak. The road ends just below the summit, where an abandoned lookout tower still stands, but it is only about a hundred-yard walk to the top, where you can see for miles in all directions. The drive itself is one of the most beautiful mountain drives in the state, and is worth a couple of hours off the main highway. Be sure to take your camera.

Winthrop is one of Washington's most popular theme towns. Leavenworth has its Bavarian theme, Lynden is Dutch, Poulsbo is Scandinavian, and Winthrop is western. It is rather fitting because the area does have a lot of cattle and hayfields, and it also was the home of Owen Wister, the novelist who wrote America's first western novel, *The Virginian*, there.

Winthrop was a sawmill and ranching town for many years, until the sawmill closed and ranching was overtaken by summer residences and tourism. The widow of the sawmill owner offered matching funds if the town wanted to adopt the western theme. So they built the false fronts and the tourists came. Now the area has one of the longest cross-country ski trails in the nation and property values continue to rise. The Winthrop tourism folks have an unusual way of describing the drive-through tourists. They are "lickers and clickers" because they stop to buy an ice-cream cone and to take a few pictures before going on their way.

Before you go on your way, take an hour or so to drive up to Sun Mountain Lodge, one of those places that is so beautiful you shouldn't miss it. The place was built on the top of a mountain so that you have a 360-degree view. It has the largest privately owned hiking and cross-country skiing trail system in the state, and it has the biggest string of saddle and pack horses.

The view from its bar is westward into the North Cascades, and a friend who lives in the area told me that sometimes when he sees a storm brewing in the Cascades, he and his wife will dash up to the Sun Mountain bar to watch it come down the mountains to the Methow valley.

From Winthrop the highway follows the Methow River south to Twisp. At this small town you have a choice of leaving State 20 and continuing south on State 153 to the Columbia River and US 97, or continuing on State 20 across the state. It swings due east just south of Twisp and enters the first range of rolling, barren hills that lies between the Cascades and the Okanogan highlands. After about thirty miles of ranches and crooked highway you arrive in the twin towns of Okanogan and Omak.

While they aren't totally connected—they are about three miles apart—the towns have grown toward each other so much that you can hardly tell the difference. They are working folks' towns more than tourist destinations, which makes them more interesting because they still have a "real" feel to them. You can find ten-penny nails and irrigation sprinklers in the hardware stores, and the price of a room in a good motel is about half what you will pay in Winthrop or Port Townsend. When restaurant menus offer steak, you will be getting a lot of meat, plus potatoes, salad, and all the coffee you dare drink. Ask for the wine list and you may or may not get one. In fact, one of the most popular places to eat is a small cafe in the Omak stockyards called the Gibson Girls Stockyard Cafe. No telephone, no reservations, just show up and have meat loaf, chicken-fried steak, or other traditional American dishes.

(See Chapter 5 for an alternate route from Okanogan.)

State 20 joins the busier US 97 in Omak and follows it north about twenty-five miles along the Okanogan River to Tonasket, where State 20 departs and heads east into the heart of the Okanogan highlands. The highlands include most of the Okanogan and Colville national forests and the Kettle River Range, a small spur of the Rocky Mountains that dribbled off into Washington from Idaho. This region is noted for cattle, pine timber, gold mines, and the ghost towns that record the history of gold mining. While the highlands aren't as high as the Cascades, still Sherman Creek Pass, at 5,575 feet, is the highest highway pass in the state.

The first town after you leave Tonasket is Wauconda, one of those rare one-building towns that has almost everything you need. It features a gas pump, a post office, a general store, and a restaurant good enough to be written up in newspapers and magazines as a destination. In addition to all of the above, the restaurant also has excellent views across the valley and low mountains.

The next town of more than one building is Republic, another one of those "real" towns that is also interesting. It is a gold-mining town—at this writing, two mines are in operation there—and it also serves ranchers, forest-service employees, loggers, and tourists. Its historical museum tells the town's boom-and-bust history. Republic's first gold rush occurred at almost exactly the same time as the Klondike discovery in 1896, and gold has been mined there off and on ever since.

The town had its share of ups and downs and promoters who came and went. Promoters in the nineteenth century were perhaps the most positive people who ever lived, and those in Republic talked endlessly of how the town would soon be a major metropolis. They also talked about a railroad that was going to come to town anytime. They talked about this one so much that it became known as the Hot Air Line. To the skeptics' chagrin, in 1902 a line was built south from Grand Forks, just across the border in British Columbia, and was soon taken over by the Great Northern line.

One room of the museum is devoted to the Stonerose fossil bed. The bed itself is at the edge of town and on private land but permission to dig is given by the volunteer staff in the museum. Most of the fossils are of leaves, including those of a rose—the so-called stone rose—that has been extinct for nobody knows how long.

From Republic the highway climbs through the beautiful pine forests and open meadows, clears Sherman Pass, and coasts down to Roosevelt Lake of the Columbia River at Kettle

27

Falls. This town is distinguished by a sign on the outskirts proclaiming its population, and below that is a smaller sign, in bold letters and suitably illustrated, proclaiming that it also has one grouch. A contest is held each year to appoint the year's grouch. Before the Columbia River dams, Kettle Falls actually was a waterfall. Like so many interesting things along the river, the falls were covered by the backwaters of Roosevelt Lake.

Another major north-south route, US 395, is crossed at Kettle Falls, but State 20 continues its eastward run, this time through the worn-down Selkirk Mountains to the tiny town of Tiger on the Pend Oreille River. This is a region of small valleys, pine-covered hillsides, and inexpensive resorts on small lakes that cater to families. You won't find many of these resorts listed in the expensive magazines because they are usually basic and reasonably priced; cabins with furniture but no bedding, woodstoves, and perhaps community showers are common. Fishing for trout and bass are popular, as is hunting for deer, elk, and black bear. You may see an occasional moose in these forests, and grizzly bears aren't common but they also wander through. Wolves and coyotes visit, and infrequently the woodland caribou herd from Idaho and southern British Columbia comes through.

The highway follows the banks of the slow, stately Pend Oreille River south to Newport on the Idaho state line, where State 20 disappears into the transcontinental US 2.

In the Area

Port Townsend Chamber of Commerce, 206-385-2722

Whidbey Island Visitors' Council, 206-675-3535

Mount Vernon Chamber of Commerce, 206-428-8547

Concrete Chamber of Commerce, 206-853-8181

North Cascades National Park, 206-856-5700

Winthrop Chamber of Commerce, 509-996-2125

Okanogan Chamber of Commerce, 509-422-0441

Omak Chamber of Commerce, 509-826-1880

Republic Chamber of Commerce, 509-775-3998

Wauconda Store, Post Office, and Restaurant, 509-486-2322

Kettle Falls Chamber of Commerce, 509-738-6514

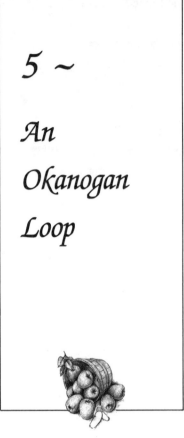

5 ~

An Okanogan Loop

In Omak, take the Conconully Road to Conconully, then on north along the Similkameen Creek to Loomis, Palmer Lake, Nighthawk, and west to Oroville. Continue east on the Oroville–Toroda Creek Road to Molson Road, turn north on it to the townsite of the three Molsons, take the dirt road out of Old Molson to Chesaw, where you'll rejoin the Oroville–Toroda Creek Road. Follow it to State 20 at Wauconda.

Highlights: *Rolling hills, farmland, orchards, lakes; Molson, a town with a fascinating legendary past; other old and remote towns.*

You'll see some of the Okanogan highland's most beautiful scenery on this long loop. Conconully is a favorite camping and picnic place for locals, and the Similkameen valley has become almost entirely orchards in the past several years. The three-Molson story is one of Washington's strangest, and Chesaw is one of the state's most remote towns.

Several years ago, on the spur of the moment, two friends and I had no plans for the Fourth of July so we picked a town at random to visit for the celebration. It was Conconully. None of us had been there and the other two hadn't even heard of the town. We drove across the Cascades and arrived in Conconully an hour or so before the fireworks began. We ate a hamburger in a tavern while watching the drama of the day-to-day life of the locals then drove about midway out Conconully Lake for the fireworks. We later agreed that it was one of the nicest Fourth of July celebrations any of us had ever had, even though not much happened. We had talked to a lot of people, including a part-time real estate agent who tried to sell us some property on the lake. I should have bought some.

This loop trip that includes Conconully begins in downtown Omak. You'd best ask directions to Conconully in case the route is marked no better than it was then, which means not at all. You have to turn west off the main drag on a street that intersects Conconully Road. It is a pretty drive out across the rolling hills that surround valleys where hay and fruit are grown. On our weekend the fields were littered with bales of hay that would soon be loaded onto semis for me to follow, very slowly, over the Cascades to the horse set along Puget Sound. Most of the hilltops have a fringe of timber, although some are completely bald.

Conconully is a very small town, no more than 200 residents, but here you will find the beautiful man-made lake with Conconully State Park on the edge of town. The town consists of the tavern we ate in, a grocery store, and a few other businesses.

A gravel road leads from Conconully north along the Similkameen Creek and valley, and passes a scattering of small lakes before arriving at Loomis. Loomis and Nighthawk are two towns with more than one life each. They were built by gold miners, then abandoned to ghost-town status, then recently revived as the area became populated and orchards were planted in the valley. Now nearly every acre that can be cultivated is planted with fruit trees and irrigated from the creek and Palmer Lake, created by a dam near Nighthawk.

Just north of Nighthawk is the Canadian border with a customs station that is open only part of the time. It is rumored to be one of the loneliest customs posts along the U.S.–Canadian border. One friend entered the United States from Canada at this point and he said the border patrolman was so lonely he wanted a conversation, while my friend was in a hurry.

I once came home across the border at Blaine in the early morning and the inspector was so tired he fell asleep while questioning me:"Where were you born?" he asked. I told him and he sat stone still, head bowed slightly. His eyes were closed. I sat there perhaps a minute, then cleared my throat loudly. His head snapped up."Where were you born?" he asked. I answered again, and this time we got through the entire routine.

The main route turns east at Nighthawk and follows the river valley down into Oroville, only a couple of miles from the Canadian border. Since gasoline is much cheaper in the United States, several large service stations have been built in Oroville for Canadian visitors. The town also has a scattering of antique shops and restaurants.

Oroville is also at the southern tip of Lake Osoyoos, which straddles the international border and is a popular camping and picnic area. Washington has established a state park on its side and Canada has resorts and summer homes on its part of the lake. You'll note on maps that in the United States the region is spelled Okanogan. Across the border it is spelled Okanagan.

In downtown Oroville, take the Oroville-Toroda Road east. It passes several apple orchards then climbs quickly to the crest of a low range of hills and twists and turns through a ravine for about eight miles to the junction with Molson Road. Take Molson Road north through the open country to the townsite of the three Molsons, home of one of Washington's most eccentric town stories.

The first Molson was built when a gold mine opened nearby, and was financed by a promoter and a scion of the Canadian Molson Brewery family. Not long after the town was founded and an elaborate hotel was built, a stranger came into town, did a little investigating, and filed a homestead claim on almost the entire town. As it turned out, Molson and his partner hadn't bothered to tend to this legality, and the stranger was within his rights. Not particularly caring what people thought of him, the stranger next built a fence around his property. One property line went right through the middle of town.

This caused some of the townspeople to build another town down the road a piece. It became New Molson, while the original site was known as Old Molson. Some stayed in Old Molson and the inevitable feud developed between them. They fought over everything, including the post office, which New Molson stole one day when the postmaster was home taking a nap. When the bank had to be moved, it was placed on a skid and pulled from place to place—depositors had to go looking for it each morning—before it finally found a nesting place. A big grand opening celebration was held and a street fight broke out. The towns even had matching automobile agencies when horseless carriages came onto the scene. If Old Molson got a Ford agency, then New Molson insisted on having one, too. The towns were like identical twins who hated each other.

The only thing they could agree on was the need for a good school. They also knew both towns couldn't afford their own so almost exactly halfway between the towns a large brick school was built and supported equally by both towns. This became known as Center Molson.

Eventually the enduring feud was settled by the absence of participants. Nearly everyone moved away, leaving Old Molson a total ghost town, and the consolidation movement closed the school. One or two families remain in New Molson, and the school building is now a museum. Nobody lives in Old Molson, and it has also become a museum with outdoor displays of farming equipment. The post office, a store building, and a handful of other business buildings remain and house exhibits.

From Molson, follow the unpaved Molson Summit Road due east (the best view for photographs of the towns is from this road when it crests the first hill) through the timber to Chesaw, which became a haven for those preferring what became known as alternate life-styles. It is quite remote, and many of its citizens are still there for the solitude, and to throw pots, write, paint, and grow much of their own food.

The road swings southeast from Chesaw to Toroda Creek Road. Follow it south to the ghost towns of Bodie and Old Toroda. There's hardly anything left of either town except one or two old wood buildings, but neither looks like a town anymore; I wouldn't have recognized them as townsites if I hadn't been told about them. The road meanders along canyons and beside creek beds and eventually joins State 20 at Wauconda.

In the Area

All phone numbers are in area code 509.

Conconully Chamber of Commerce, 826-0813

Okanogan Chamber of Commerce, 422-0441

Tonasket Chamber of Commerce, 486-2931

6 ~

Inside

Hood

Canal

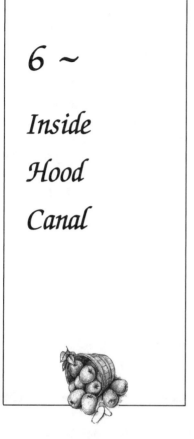

From Belfair on State 3: Take State 300 west. Turn left at Tahuya onto the gravel road to Dewatto and stay on it through Holly to Seabeck and State 3 again.

Highlights: *The quiet beauty of Hood Canal, views of the Olympics, tree farms, and quiet tideflats.*

First, an alert (I prefer that word over the more dire "warning"): In no place in Washington is the property-ownership impulse—perhaps the territorial imperative would be more accurate—more visible than along the shores of Hood Canal. More private property signs are posted along the waterfront there than in any other place I have ever visited. These people do not want you walking on their turf and you have no choice but to take them seriously.

Unlike Oregon and a few other enlightened states, Washington permits people to own beaches and tidelands, and most of these owners are protective of their property to the extreme. Example: A few years ago a friend and I packed a picnic lunch and drove down Hood Canal looking for a likely place to park our hamper and enjoy the sun, light breeze, and views of the mountains. We found a tideflat with a place to park beside the road, a well-used trail, and no "Private Property" signs. We had our picnic laid out on a stump, the wine opened, and the potato salad sampled, when a woman with a serious expression and a notebook came down the trail and demanded our names ("I already have your license number so you had just as well give me your names because I can get them anyway"). We didn't give her our names, but we did leave.

With this unpleasantness out of the way, you can enjoy Hood Canal without getting into real-estate disputes by sticking to the obviously public areas, such as Belfair State Park, and designated picnic areas in the towns along the route.

Hood Canal is not actually a canal. It is an eighty-mile-long arm of Puget Sound with a sharp hook on the southern end. It comes awfully close to meeting the rest of Puget Sound at its very tip; there are no more than two miles between the canal and the northern tip of Case Inlet. You can rest assured that if it had been commercially practical, or if it ever will be, the canal will be built. Although its narrow configuration might lead you to think it was mistaken for a canal by the explorers, it actually was named Hood's Channel by Captain George Vancouver in 1792 in honor of Lord Hood of the Admiralty Board. Someone entered it on Vancouver's charts as Hood's Canal, and eventually it became Hood Canal. Nobody seems to know why.

Although it is easiest to find public places along US 101 (described in Chapter 7), my favorite trip along the canal is along the shoreline on the inside of the hook. This route is less traveled, and the road is not paved much of the way.

At Belfair on State 3, turn west on State 300 toward Belfair State Park and Tahuya. The road is busy during the summer months because Belfair State Park is so popular. If you didn't buy your picnic supplies in Belfair, you can stop at the store across the road from the state park. This will be your last chance for food or gasoline until you reach Holly.

The road stays close to the shore most of the way to Tahuya with peek-a-boo views of the salt water through the houses and trees. The road is generally slow because it is crooked and nobody is in a hurry, anyway. The canal has its own special beauty, especially on the quiet mornings when a fog hangs over it until the sun burns it off. On these mornings there is no wind to ruffle the surface. Birds create perfect reflections as they fly only inches off the water, and a jumping fish makes almost as much noise as a beaver slapping its tail on the water.

The Hood Canal

Not until you reach Tahuya will the views be really spectacular because that is where the Olympics make their appearance. Tahuya is a very small town, and if you ask around you will probably find a place to picnic without threat of arrest.

Just after you leave town, the timber is so dense that you'll feel as though you're entering a cave. From here to Dewatto you are driving on a basic country road, steep in places, narrow most of the time, and muddy in wet weather. You'll find a few wide spots where you can pull over to the side and admire the views. But even though you are away from the water, and in places several hundred feet above sea level, you'll still be greeted by "Private Property" signs.

After about eight miles of driving up and down and around sharp curves, you will find that the road drops back down to relatively level land and is in a bit better condition. Then it abruptly reaches a T-junction. Turn left and you'll soon be on the tideflats of Dewatto Creek. Turn left at the road by the creek bridge and it will lead you down to the almost-ghost-town of Dewatto, a place being constantly rediscovered by people wanting a rural experience.

The place was named by the local Native Americans, who didn't like it at all. They avoided it entirely. They called it *Du-a-ta*, meaning "place where the evil spirits come out of the earth." They believed these spirits, named *Tub-ta-ba*, entered people's bodies and drove them crazy. Some antidevelopment folks would probably like for the stories to be resurrected.

Beyond Dewatto the road leaves the shore again and climbs out of the old-growth timberland into an area that was logged off many years ago. The first time I drove the road in 1979, the new trees weren't much larger than a standard Christmas tree. A decade later the trees are a forest, still not large enough to be cut but large enough to remind me of what an emotional issue logging is, even when it occurs on private property. No matter how hard timber companies try to convince the public that trees are a crop (and let's be honest, they are), few of us can equate trees with corn and peas and boysenberries. As the philosopher said, "Go figure."

After climbing gradually for several miles on the washboardy road that feels sunken because the banks on either side are so high and the trees are now so tall, you finally reach the crest and begin an ascent toward the salt water again. At the bottom of the hill, take a left turn to Holly, a small town that once was quite remote and a popular place for summer homes. Today it is part of the suburbia that is creeping across the Kitsap Peninsula and around Hood Canal. From here, the highway takes you to Seabeck and Puget Sound.

In the Area

Belfair State Park, 206-478-4625

7 ~

US 101

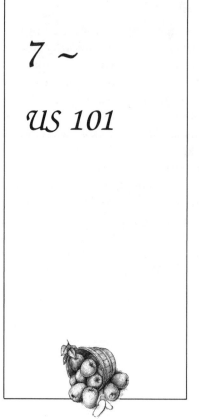

From Astoria-Megler toll bridge: Take US 101 north all the way around the Olympic Peninsula. The famous coastal highway that begins in San Diego terminates when it merges with I-5 in Olympia.

Highlights: *The best that the Olympic Peninsula can offer: the Columbia River estuary, cranberry bogs, several wildlife refuges, beautiful lakes, the Olympic National Park's coastal strip and rain forest, and Hood Canal.*

Calling a major U.S. highway a country road may seem to stretch the definition beyond the breaking point, but this is the highway that takes you entirely around the Olympic Peninsula, and much of it feels and looks like country road. The Olympic Peninsula is relatively undeveloped—thanks to the Olympic National Park, Olympic National Forest, and the Quinault, Makah, Shoalwater, and Quillayute Indian reservations. It also has some of the most rugged landscape you'll find in the country without going to Alaska.

If you think you can "do" the Olympic Peninsula in only two days, you'll be disappointed. Although it is only a bit more than 300 miles from Grays Harbor around to Olympia, you should allow yourself three days minimum. Trust me; I speak from experience.

US 101 comes within only 50 miles of making a complete loop during its 300-plus-mile sojourn through Washington; that is the distance from Aberdeen at the foot of the Olympic Peninsula to the highway's terminus at Olympia.

The route, which travels from north to south, begins at the north side of the Columbia River at the Astoria-Megler toll bridge. From the bridge the highway runs northwest along the bank of the vast river estuary. Here it is so broad that it looks more like the open ocean than a river mouth.

Much of Fort Columbia was buried in a low headland, out of reach of enemy artillery. Now a state park, it began as an army fort to protect the northern side of the entrance to the Columbia River. Like Fort Stevens, its counterpart on the Oregon side, Fort Columbia was equipped with cannons, called disappearing rifles (see Chapter 4 for more information). It never fired a shot in anger and was eventually abandoned and donated to the state. The park is small and modest and is greatly overshadowed by Fort Stevens, which is much larger and is one of Oregon's most heavily used parks. Part of the reason Fort Columbia has such a low profile is the large number of other things to do, and other large parks with better views and beaches, in the immediate area.

For several decades the area from Chinook to Ilwaco was one of the richest commercial salmon-fishing areas in the world. The salmon came into the shallow waters on their way upriver to their spawning streams, and the fishermen were waiting for them with long nets that were pulled out into the shallow water by horses. When the net was extended to its full length, the horses pulled each end to shore, bringing thousands of salmon and other fish onto dry land. Enormous salmon canneries were built here and in Astoria across the river and upstream at Knappton, Altoona, Pillar Rock, and other sites. The salmon were so thick that people honestly believed they could never catch them all, that the salmon would keep coming to the river forever, that they were a renewable resource, like rain, that needed no help to keep replenishing itself. It didn't take long before people were predicting an end to the salmon supply, but it almost took too long for the government to do anything about it. Today the salmon is perhaps the world's most heavily subsidized creature.

During those years when horse-drawn nets were used, fishermen also built large fish traps along the shore that directed the homeward-bound fish into an enclosed area where they could be bailed out into waiting boats. It has been said that at one time Chinook, Washington, was the wealthiest town in America on a per capita basis. This eventually ended when the salmon runs were almost depleted and the large nets and fish traps were outlawed. Some fishermen still work out of Chinook and Ilwaco, but the industry is more a memory than a reality today. Commercial fishing boats share the marinas with salmon and bottom-fish charter boats.

Just outside Ilwaco is a cluster of attractions worth a detour. First is Fort Canby State Park, a large park with lots of room for camping. It also has some of the best beaches, walking trails, and viewpoints in the area.

On around the estuary a short distance, at the base of Cape Disappointment, is the U.S. Coast Guard's National Motor Lifeboat School. This is where the coxswains of those tough, fast surfboats are trained, and the site was selected because it has more days of rough water than anywhere else outside Alaska. The coxswains are trained to operate the lifeboats that are so tough that they can flip over in the surf, right themselves, and keep going. Crewmen are strapped on to these boats and veterans of overturns say it is incredibly noisy under water, and that although it usually takes less than thirty seconds for the boat to right itself, it seems like hours. The school's informal motto is: "You have to go out but you don't have to come back," meaning that when a life is in danger, they go out. No exceptions. As a testament to their training, very few men and women working on the lifeboats are ever injured and, as this was being written in 1993, it has been nearly thirty years since a life was lost.

Sometimes you can watch them from the North Head lighthouse as they go through their lifesaving drills. If they're working particularly close to the shore, where the surf is heaviest, you can see them from the North Jetty of the river. Another viewpoint is from the Lewis and Clark Interpretive Center atop the cape.

The Lewis and Clark center was built to commemorate the arrival of the explorers in November 1805, the first overland party to cross America: Captain Meriwether Lewis had traveled from Washington, D.C., which made him the first American to go from coast to coast overland. Originally the party intended to camp on the north side of the river, but when the travelers tried to set up camp they didn't like the exposed area, and food on the hoof—deer and elk—was too far away. So they paddled across the river and settled on a site back in the woods on a small river where they had shelter from the winter storms and where deer and elk weren't so distant. The interpretive center tells the story of the expedition and offers one of the best views of the coast from its aerie high on the cape.

Although US 101 swings inland around Willapa Bay and misses the Long Beach Peninsula, this is one of the state's most popular beach areas. It has excellent hotels and inns,

North Head Light

two or three of the better restaurants in the state, interesting historical towns such as Oysterville, several good artists who sell their work direct to the public, and an incredibly long beach with room for thousands of visitors. The onshore wind is almost constant, so kite flying is one of the most popular activities. In addition to recreation, this area is also known for its cranberry bogs and oyster farms.

The highway stays close to Willapa Bay most of the way north to South Bend and Raymond. The bay is shallow and during low tides you will see miles and miles of mudflats with all manner of patterns created by the receding water.

At Raymond the highway swings inland through hilly country and forests that are mostly owned by timber companies. The highway occasionally has turnout lanes for logging trucks and recreational vehicles but like most of US 101, the driving is at a modest speed.

The tri-cities of Cosmopolis, Aberdeen, and Hoquiam are clustered around the eastern end of Grays Harbor, another large natural harbor that, until the spotted owl controversy, was one of the state's busiest ports for log exporting. The bay is sheltered from the ocean by peninsulas of sand that have built up over the centuries around the entrance in the middle. The southern peninsula features the commercial and sportfishing town of Westport, and the northern peninsula cradles the resort community of Ocean Shores.

US 101 doesn't show you much of the harbor and it leaves Hoquiam and heads north into the heart of the Olympic Peninsula, avoiding the coastal communities of Ocean Shores, Ocean City, Copalis Beach, Pacific Beach, and Moclips. The latter town is the farthest you can drive on this road, unless you are a member of the Quinault tribe or have special permission to enter the Quinault Reservation. Tired of encroachments by non-Native Americans, the Quinaults closed State 109 at the reservation boundary in the late 1960s.

US 101 is mostly an avenue through the forest. You'll first go through privately owned forest, then national forest land until you reach Lake Quinault on the southern edge of Olympic National Park. This large lake is the source of the Quinault River and has excellent fishing and boating. Lake Quinault Lodge is the most popular place on the lake, and it is one of those ancient wooden lodges that remind you of more gracious eras and cars that had to be cranked to be started. It is a sister to Klaloch Lodge to the north right on the ocean.

From Quinault Lake you can go back into the national park to trailheads that lead into the rain forest that is the ecological signature of the Olympic Peninsula. The temperate rain forest here is one of only three in the entire world (the others are in Chile and New Zealand), and it is an odd sensation to walk through the dense forest between and beneath trees virtually dripping with moss, yet in gentle temperatures that hover around 50 degrees. It is the silence of this forest that strikes visitors, in addition to the lush scenery, of course. If moss doesn't literally drip, the skies do. More than 200 inches (that's more than 16 feet) of rainfall is recorded here each year. Bring your rain gear.

From Quinault the highway swings back to the west and reaches the coast eight miles later at Queets, a small village on the northern boundary of the Quinault Reservation. Here the coastal strip of Olympic National Park begins and continues far to the north at La Push. This strip was controversial when it was added by President Franklin D. Roosevelt in the late 1930s, and still is controversial among those who would like to log all the timber of the peninsula.

However, the national park has preserved the beach in its wild state, and one of the most popular hikes in the state is along the ocean beach. Some hikers complete the entire strip between where the highway leaves the beach at the Hoh River

Along the Washington coast

to Ozette, a distance of about forty-six miles. Most hike it in two or three stages; hiking on the beaches is hard going if you have to walk in loose sand with a heavy pack, and you must plan your hike around the tides to avoid being stranded on a headland or rock by the high tide.

This stretch of highway is one of the most beautiful in the state, and some travelers say it features the most dramatic scenery along the entire length of US 101, from California north. The coast is very rugged, with hundreds of offshore rocks that are home for marine mammals and birds. The forest along here has never been logged, so most of it is the way nature designed it. Several trails lead from the highway down to the beach. Ruby Beach is a particular favorite with photographers. Other trails lead back into the main part of the national park, to the Hoh Rain Forest, and other points of interest.

After following the coast for awhile, the highway heads back inland again at the Hoh River, then swings around north past the Bogachiel River State Park and along the bank of the Bogachiel River. The river is notable for its sea-run cutthroat trout and winter steelhead runs.

The next town is Forks, one of the state's most famous towns even though its population is only about 3,000. Forks is the ultimate logging town; until the emergence of the spotted owl as an indicator for loss of wildlife habitat, nearly everyone who lived in Forks was involved in some way with logging. The decline in logging has forced its citizens to cast about for other sources of income, but the rugged individualism it is known for still thrives.

Forks has several legendary events and characters in its past, and my favorite is what happened when a famous motorcycle club arrived one holiday weekend, intent on taking over the town. The police were outnumbered and the town was too isolated to get immediate help from other sources. So the fire department was called out and it joined the police force in battling the bikers.

The citizenry soon had enough of this nonsense. Things were really getting rough, so dozens of loggers jumped in and helped evict the gang without worrying too much about the gang's civil rights. Soon US 101 was filled with motorcycles heading south.

It wasn't as though the police never had trouble with the loggers. Some of the loggers had been thrown in jail by the police during Friday or Saturday night brawls. But this was different.

"We don't like for our cops to get bent," was how one citizen described the reasoning behind joining the policemen and firemen in the brawl.

A road leads from Forks down to the coastal town of La Push on the small Quillayute Indian Reservation. The town has an excellent beach and this is the entrance to the

Quillayute Needles National Wildlife Refuge and the Washington Islands Wilderness Area. All offshore rocks along the coast are designated national wildlife refuges to provide habitat for birds and sea mammals. Consequently you cannot climb on them.

The campground at La Push is a good place to launch long hikes in either direction. To the north is the spectacular Rialto Beach and south are the unimaginatively named but beautiful Second and Third beaches. If you only want a good day hike, you can hike either direction to the first headland, climb it for a view of the coastline, then return to your car at La Push.

Shortly after leaving Forks, the highway takes a swing around to the east for its run through the forest to the small town of Sappho and continues on to Lake Crescent, which many consider the most beautiful lake on the Olympic Peninsula, if not in the entire state. Even though US 101 runs along its southern shore and logging trucks scare the bejesus out of dawdling tourists, the lake is surrounded by such beautiful mountains and there are so few developments on its shores (most of it is owned by the Olympic National Park) that it is very easy to forget that it isn't out in the wilderness alone.

Three lodges lie along the lake, and you will find several places to pull off the highway for a breather or short hike. One of the best views in the area is from atop Pyramid Peak on the northwestern shore, a hike that takes between two and three hours from the lake. During World War II an aircraft spotter station was built atop the peak, and from this perch you can see far back into the Olympics and north across the Strait of Juan de Fuca to Canada.

Another nice hike that will take less than an hour is to Marymeer Falls, only a short distance from the highway on a fairly level trail.

The highway skirts Lake Sutherland a short distance east of Crescent, then drops down into Port Angeles, the largest town on the peninsula. Here you can catch the ferry M/V *Coho* to Victoria, British Columbia, and you can stop in at the Olympic National Park headquarters on the edge of town. A good side trip is to Hurricane Ridge, which gives you a helicopterlike view into the heart of the Olympic Mountains and most of the Strait of Juan de Fuca with Vancouver Island and Victoria in the background.

The country-road aspect of US 101 disappears at Port Angeles as the traffic increases markedly and commercial development takes over from here to Hood Canal. It is interesting to note that only a short distance from where the annual rainfall is more than sixteen feet you will cross through the rain-shadow effect at Sequim, where the Olympic Mountains rob nearly all the clouds of their rain, leaving only ten inches or less for the area in line with the rain-robbing peaks. This has made the small town of Sequim particularly attractive to retirees who want a mild climate without getting their feet wet. Several retirement homes and communities have sprung up around the small but rapidly growing town.

The highway next skirts the southern end of Discovery Bay and heads almost due south along the western shore of Hood Canal. Several state parks and marinas are located along this stretch, but the traffic is so heavy that the silence of the trip described in Chapter 6 is missing. Still, it is a beautiful drive with many places to turn off for walks and picnics, on public land in state parks where you'll be safe from the territorial imperative.

After leaving Hood Canal, US 101 speeds along to Shelton, a sawmill town that is also seeking additional sources of jobs. The town has a beautiful setting on a long, narrow hook of Puget Sound called Hammersley Inlet. The area is perhaps best known for its Christmas tree industry. Each winter more than 3 million trees are cut, packaged, and shipped all over America.

US 101 continues south and east to join State 8 just before it reaches I-5 on the edge of Olympia.

In the Area

All phone numbers are in area code 206.

Long Beach Peninsula Association, 642-4421

Grays Harbor Chamber of Commerce, 532-1924

Forks Chamber of Commerce, 374-2531

Olympic National Park, 452-4501

Lake Quinault Lodge, 288-2571

Port Angeles Chamber of Commerce, 452-2363

Sequim Chamber of Commerce, 683-6197

Shelton Chamber of Commerce, 426-2021

8 ~

Through the Heart of Lewis County

From I-5 at Chehalis: Take State 6 west and turn south on State 603 through Napavine and Winlock to Vader. Turn west on State 506 to Ryderwood and Boistfort, and rejoin State 6 at Pe Ell. Follow it to US 101 at Raymond.

Highlights: *Lush farming and dairy lands; a unique retirement town, the state's most unusual state park and Willipa Bay.*

This is the kind of countryside where you'll see the names of the local high school teams proudly displayed in the towns and on car bumpers. Although the larger towns, such as Chehalis, are steadily growing and creating suburbs far out into the countryside, the whole area retains its bucolic atmosphere.

Start this loop trip from the north, beginning at Chehalis by driving west on State 6 a short distance to State 603, which heads south to Napavine and Winlock. Most of the scenery to Napavine is given over to newer homes built along the highway, although occasionally you can see Mount Rainier and

Mount St. Helens on clear days. Once you reach Napavine, the houses thin out and the scenery becomes more rural with lots of dairy cattle munching back and forth across the low hills in meadows cleared from the fir and hemlock forest.

In the middle of Winlock you will see an enormous egg with a sign proclaiming it the biggest egg in the world. My first thought was that I would hate to meet a bird that could lay one that large. Fear not: It is made of reinforced concrete. It is there because while the main north-south highway, US 99, was being built, all towns between Seattle and Portland were asked to participate in the opening celebration with a float. In those days of few automobiles highway construction was a big news event, unlike today when traffic is so heavy that when construction workers take down the barricades they must run for their lives. Winlock was in the egg business in a big way then, so the town created a gigantic papier-mâché egg to put on a float. Since it made a big hit in the parade, a collection was taken up to build an even larger egg, this one of concrete, and it was placed on wooden poles with a sign proclaiming Winlock as the "Egg Capital of the World."

Some years later, as if the Humpty Dumpty story had to be authenticated, the poles rotted and collapsed, dropping the egg to the ground and smashing it into many pieces. By this time Winlock was no longer noted in the egg business but the town took up another collection and built another egg, of plastic this time, and placed it on a pedestal near the railroad.

Several years ago when I first drove this road, I was pleasantly surprised to see that someone had placed a set of signs along the road in honor of the old Burma-Shave signs. In case you are too young to have ever seen those signs, they were stationed along America's highways for nearly forty years; the first went up in 1925 and they stopped putting them

53

up in 1963. Most consisted of five lines, with the fifth line always reading, "Burma-Shave."

So when I saw the reincarnated Burma-Shave signs near Vader that read:

> They missed the turn
> Car was whizz'n
> Fault was her'n
> Funeral his'n
> Burma-Shave

I took out one of my favorite books, *Verse by the Side of the Road* by Frank Rowsome, and went through again to read my favorites, suffering a serious attack of nostalgia for the days when I owned a canary yellow 1946 Ford convertible and waited anxiously for the next set of Burma-Shave signs.

These are some of my favorites:

> Slow down, Pa
> Sakes alive
> Ma missed signs
> Four
> And five.

> She kissed
> The hairbrush
> By mistake
> She thought it was
> Her husband Jake

> If you think
> She likes
> Your bristles
> Walk bare-footed
> Through some thistles

Thirty days
Hath September
April
June and the
Speed offender

The resurrected Burma-Shave signs put me in the proper frame of mind for the small town of Ryderwood. Seventy-some years ago, when the Long-Bell Lumber Company went into the business of cutting down trees in the area and sawing them into logs and boards, the company had to build its own towns here and there for its employees. Ryderwood was one of them. When Long-Bell went out of business, some of the towns remained and some were abandoned. Ryderwood was one that stayed alive, and it did so by becoming a retirement village.

It isn't at all inactive, though. I was once sent there by a newspaper for a story on the town and everyone was so busy with various projects and interests that we could hardly get anyone to talk to us. Our original plan was to line up every-one in town for a group photo, but that was totally out of the question. They just weren't interested, and most didn't care if their names and pictures were in the paper at all. It was an attitude I found refreshing after being pursued by people desperate for public attention. We got a story but it wasn't much, the editor told us.

With the memory of that event fresh in mind, when I last drove through Ryderwood, I did so only to refresh my visual memory, and as before, hardly anybody was on the street and no tricycles or other indications of young people were show-ing. I did see some people working in their gardens and on roofs, but I didn't see anyone sitting on the front porch doing nothing.

From Ryderwood the road becomes almost a boulevard between dairy farms, and nearly every farm I passed had some kind of dairy award noted or posted on the fences, by the mailboxes, or at the gates. Some of the houses and farm buildings are right beside the highway as though the farmers didn't want to waste good farmland on things like lawns, but I suspect that the buildings are in their original places and the highway widened.

At the small village of Boistfort the main road goes almost due north back to State 6, but west is a prettier drive on the smaller, quieter paved road to the town of Pe Ell. It began life as Pierre, but local legend has it that the Native Americans living in the area couldn't pronounce the *r*'s in *Pierre* and called it something like Pe Ell, so the name stuck.

Cows munch contentedly

The next town has a similar story. The founder of Lebam had a daughter named Mabel. He reversed the spelling when it came time to name the town. I hope Mabel thought it was funny.

From Lebam it is an easy drive on in to Raymond and US 101, but you should make one more stop and pay homage to the man whose grave constitutes Washington's tiniest state park. It is Willie Keil's Grave State Park. It is a grave with a strange story.

Willie Keil was the nineteen-year-old son of William Keil, a Prussian who came to America around 1800 as a tailor. This was the era of Christian communism, and all over Europe and North America Christian and Utopian communes were formed, some quite successful. William Keil was the founder of a group that settled in Bethel, Missouri, a short distance west of Hannibal. The commune was successful and its members became very wealthy. When the Oregon fever struck America in the 1840s, the commune, by now called the Bethelites, was also afflicted with the fever, and it was decided that a group of its members should go forth and start a new commune in the Oregon Country.

Dr. William Keil decided to lead the group. Young Willie was probably the most excited member of the party, but a short time before the expedition left he fell ill with malaria. As he lay dying, he hallucinated and sometimes believed he was at the head of the wagon train, leading the group across the plains and mountains. During his lucid moments, he pleaded with his parents to promise that he could go with them.

Soon the boy died and the parents set about keeping their promise to him. They had a casket built with a lead lining and filled it with alcohol and placed the boy's body in it. They loaded the casket onto a wagon Keil had built especially to carry the ill boy. Now it was made into a hearse. All the way across the plains and mountains to the Oregon Country the hearse wagon led the party.

Word went ahead via the moccasin telegraph of the unusual procession, and they were left alone by the Indians who liked to prey on wagon trains. However, the Blackfeet tribe didn't know about the Bethelites and one night they stole some cattle from the procession. Before long the cattle were back; other tribes had told the Blackfeet about the hearse and that was enough to make the Blackfeet believe the travelers should be left alone.

When the group reached Willapa Bay they established a village and held a decent burial for Willie on a hillside with a view to the north. The Bethelites soon realized that they had not selected a good place for a town—too remote and too damp—so they packed up and moved to a site not far south of Portland. They named it Aurora in honor of the Keils' daughter, and the town still stands, as does its sister town, Bethel, Missouri.

In the Area

Raymond Chamber of Commerce, 206-942-5419

9 ~

Down the Columbia to the Sea

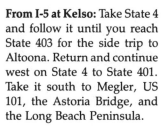

From I-5 at Kelso: Take State 4 and follow it until you reach State 403 for the side trip to Altoona. Return and continue west on State 4 to State 401. Take it south to Megler, US 101, the Astoria Bridge, and the Long Beach Peninsula.

Highlights: *Broad Columbia River with its oceangoing traffic, sloughs with anchored log booms, Columbia white-tailed deer refuge, picturesque river towns, Long Beach Peninsula, and the Pacific Ocean.*

Locally this route is called the Ocean Beach Highway for the simple and obvious reason that it is the route people in the Longview-Kelso area take to the Long Beach Peninsula. It is a beautiful highway; I drove it perhaps a hundred times when I lived in Longview, and have found reasons to drive it several times during the past few years. I still haven't found a dull mile.

The Lower Columbia River is almost an arm of the Pacific Ocean because it is subject to the ebb and flow of the tides. This effect can be seen and felt all the way upstream to the Bonneville Dam in the Columbia Gorge. The tidal flow is so strong that tugboats towing barges or log booms must move with the tide because a heavily loaded tug sometimes cannot move at all when the tide is running out, letting the river run free. They must wait until the tide reaches its peak and stops running or they can time their trips to coincide with the tidal flow going in their direction.

The Columbia is dredged constantly to keep a channel deep enough for oceangoing ships, and this ship traffic gives the river a maritime look. It can be disconcerting when you are driving along the highway and suddenly see an enormous ship only a few feet away from you, looking as incongruous as an elephant down by the pond.

The highway follows the river closely for the first several miles and doesn't really leave it until it reaches the county line between Cowlitz and Wahkiakum counties. Here a long beach has been developed by dredge spoils, the sand and dirt pumped ashore from the dredges. The beach is popular with fishermen, who cast their lures far out into the river, then attach their rods to various clamps and racks. They hang a bell or other signaling device to the tip of the rod and then go about their social life, one ear always cocked for the bell while they drink coffee, stoke the beach fire, or watch television in their RVs. Because these fishing spots are so popular with retired men and women, many share the generic name of Social Security Beach.

The first town of any size downriver from Longview is Cathlamet, the county seat of Wahkiakum County. It is one of the oldest towns on the Columbia River and was founded by a former Hudson's Bay employee named Birnie. He befriended several American soldiers stationed upriver at Vancouver Barracks, which replaced Fort Vancouver when the international boundary between Canada and the United States was established. Among the soldiers was a lonely lieutenant with a drinking problem named Ulysses S. Grant, who made several trips downriver to visit Birnie.

Cathlamet has remained genuinely historical with several of the old homes and business buildings restored and occupied by hotels, bed and breakfasts, and restaurants. The town was built on a hilly piece of land overlooking Puget Island, which is the only inhabited island in the Columbia River. While most Cathlamet residents are descendants of Scandinavian and Finnish parents, many Puget Islanders are second- and third-generation Swiss. The island's industry is about evenly divided between dairy farming and commercial fishing

Along the Columbia River

with one or two small commercial fishing-boat builders thrown in. The island is laced by several canals where commercial fishing boats are moored.

Puget Island is connected to Cathlamet by a bridge tall enough to let fishing boats through. The main channel runs between the island and Oregon and it is connected to Oregon by a small car ferry. This is the only place the Columbia can be crossed between Longview and the four-mile-long Astoria-Megler bridge.

Just downstream from Cathlamet you will enter the recently renamed Julia Butler Hansen National Wildlife Refuge. Originally it was named for the Columbian white-tailed deer, an endangered subspecies of their larger white-tailed cousins now found only on this refuge and some of the islands in the river. State 4 goes along the edge of the refuge, but for the best views of the small deer and the birds that frequent the refuge, turn off the main highway at the refuge entrance and drive along a dike road through the refuge. The road rejoins State 4 at the town of Skamokawa.

Skamokawa is one of the more picturesque of the Columbia River towns. It was built where Skamokawa Creek empties into the Columbia and served as a stop for river steamboats for many years. *Skamokawa* reportedly was a local Native American word meaning "smoke on the water," because fog frequently hangs over the creek that snakes down from the foothills through the valley. Because Skamokawa Creek is lined with houses and docks, like a canal, it is inevitable that some people call it Little Venice.

The most familiar building in Skamokawa is the Redmen Hall, built several feet above the highway on a steep hillside at the east end of the bridge. Redmen was a fraternal organization several decades ago that gradually disappeared, leaving the striking building behind. It has since been taken over by the town as a community center and museum.

After Skamokawa the highway swings away from the river and goes back into the forest, climbs over the low summit of KM Mountain, and drops back down to the Grays River valley. The town of Grays River was built at the crossing of the small, flat river that meanders through the pastureland. Grays River once had a dairy cooperative processing plant and a general store, but it has been steadily dwindling until almost nothing is left. It undoubtedly will follow the pattern of other towns in Washington that have faded, then returned to life in another form.

Only a short distance west of town is the Grays River covered bridge, standing over the narrow river, looking rather forlorn out in the pasture land below the highway. It is the only covered bridge still in use in Washington, and its weight load has diminished to the point that trucks can't use it. Local history buffs keep it in working order.

At the one- or two-building town of Rosburg, treat yourself to a pleasant few minutes by taking State 403 south to the Columbia River. The blacktop road twists and turns its way along the edge of the low hills and follows the banks of Grays River into Grays Bay, a broad arm of the Columbia River. The road goes along the east side of the bay to the Columbia, then takes a sharp left turn to go up the Columbia River to Conttardi and Altoona, then to Pillar Rock about four miles farther upriver on a dirt road. These towns began as large salmon canneries built on stilts above the river so fishing boats could offload directly onto the cannery floors. They also built stores on the stilts, and small houses for workers were built on the narrow shelf of land beneath the bluffs, barely leaving room for a road to go between the river and the houses.

Little is left of the towns today because they gradually rotted away and fell into the river, but enough remains to get an idea of what once was a major industry. For decades the towns were isolated; no roads penetrated the area until well after World War II. The only transportation obviously was by boat, and regular passenger service was offered by boat companies. The companies built small buildings as waiting rooms at the head of small rivers and creeks and residents came down to catch the passenger boats in their own canoes or rowboats.

Across Grays Bay to the west lie the remains of the town named Frankfort. You may or may not be able to drive down to it, depending on conditions of the Crown Zellerback logging road, which leads to the town. Frankfort was constructed when locals were convinced that a railroad was going to be built down the Columbia from the main line that ran from Portland to Seattle. A nice town was erected on the point where the Grays River enters the Columbia, but the railroad went down the Oregon side of the river, leaving Frankfort isolated; at that time no highway went down the river. Families used the homes as summer residences for a few years and gradually stopped coming. I haven't been there in several years but I have been told some of the houses still stand, but all have been stripped of everything of value.

After driving back to Rosburg, you will go through more forest and along the Naselle River until you come to the town of Naselle. Here you can follow State 4 on to its intersection with US 101 beside Willapa Bay, or turn south in Naselle on State 401, which leads back down to the Columbia River, the Astoria-Megler Bridge, and on around the giant estuary to Chinook, Ilwaco, and the Long Beach Peninsula.

In the Area

All phone numbers are in area code 206.

Cathlamet Commercial Club, 795-8651

Julia Butler Hansen National Wildlife Refuge, 795-3912

10 ~

A Gifford Pinchot Excursion

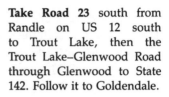

Take Road 23 south from Randle on US 12 south to Trout Lake, then the Trout Lake–Glenwood Road through Glenwood to State 142. Follow it to Goldendale.

Highlights: *Some of the best views of Mount St. Helens and Mount Adams available, secluded lakes, dense forest, remote small towns, and open cattle country.*

When Mount St. Helens blew its top on Sunday, May 18, 1980, killed fifty-nine persons, and created a wasteland of fallen trees covered with ashes, the first version of this book was sitting on the printing presses waiting for the printers to come back to work on Monday and complete the press run. Oddly, when I heard that the mountain had blown laterally rather than vertically and had leveled thousands of square acres of Gifford Pinchot National Forest, my first thought was not about the fate of the book but of the road that runs from US 12 at Randle south to Trout Lake near the Columbia Gorge. I was specifically concerned about Burley Mountain, one of my favorite viewpoints in the Cascades.

I have always liked the drive from US 12 to Trout Lake. The road is paved all the way through the forest, and it goes so close to Mount Adams that you will almost swear you can hit it with a rock. However, the map doesn't lie; the mountain is still twenty miles away.

One of the many bonuses of the route is the short side trip to the top of Burley Mountain, which offers my favorite view of all four volcanoes—Mount Rainier, Mount Adams, Mount Hood in Oregon, and, of course, Mount St. Helens, which is the closest. To my relief, a Gifford Pinchot National Forest ranger told me that Burley Mountain still stood unscathed and still had the best view of Mount St. Helens. I had hoped to go down and check the mountain for myself, but this is being written in late winter and the road will be covered with deep snow for another two or three months.

The main route under discussion here follows Forest Service Road 23 all the way and, unlike some government roads in remote places, this one is well marked at each intersection. Sometimes it degenerates down to a single lane with wide spots so cars and trucks may peacefully coexist on it, but most of it is two-lane blacktop.

To see the view from atop Burley Mountain, take Road 23 south from Randle, then turn right off Road 23 on the spur to Tower Rock Campground and continue along it to the Burley Mountain sign. The dirt road consists of seven miles of switchbacks through thick timber before it emerges on top and straightens out a bit as it follows the contour of ridges. The 5,300-foot summit of Burley Mountain sports the remains of an old lookout tower. The road continues southward and drops back down into the forest and eventually merges with a main route through the forest, but I haven't taken this road. I recommend having a good, long look around at the summit to admire the four volcanoes and to be glad you weren't standing there when the mountain exploded, creating 300-mile-an-hour winds that carried temperatures of more than 300 degrees across the forest.

Until this happened, Mount St. Helens was almost a perfect cone and was sometimes called America's Mount Fuji. Spirit Lake at its northeast base was a popular camping area and millions of photographs had been taken of the mountain reflected in the lake. In March 1980, the mountain began a series of small eruptions, steam and ash puffs that rose several thousand feet in the air. More ominously, the eastern side of the mountain began bulging, and scientists on the site knew it was only a matter of time before the mountain would literally blow its top. It did so at 8:32 that May morning. The blast took 1,400 feet off the mountain and the ash cloud climbed 16 miles into the sky and drifted east, bringing darkness at noon to many eastern Washington towns—Yakima, Moses Lake, Ritzville, Spokane, and parts of Idaho and Montana.

Ashes covered everything, and the hardest hit town was Ritzville, where you can still see ash piled along the roadsides. One resident said he heard the ash cloud was on the way when he got ready for church that morning. He placed a newspaper on his driveway and anchored it with rocks so he could perhaps catch some of the ashes. When he came back from church the ashes were so deep he couldn't find the newspaper. Several of my friends were trapped in a Grange hall for several hours because the ash cloud was too thick to drive through.

The positive side of the experience for them was that although the ashes had a high obsidian (glass) content and were very hard on machinery, the ash enriched the soil and crops since have benefited from this unexpected and unwelcome natural fertilizer.

The eruption created enormous flash floods of melted snow and ice that swept down the mountainside into small rivers that became big rivers and eventually emptied into the Columbia River. The flood brought an apocalyptic burden of sand and rocks that filled the Cowlitz and Columbia rivers. Ship traffic was halted on the Columbia until dredges, working around the clock, could open the channels again. Major tributaries, such as the Cowlitz River, were also clogged and bridges damaged. When you drive on I-5 in the area, you'll see mounds of debris along the highway that were dredged from the river in the summer of 1980.

One of the nicest views from the Burley Mountain summit is of the series of mountains that are different shades of blue depending on their distance from you. They undulate off into the distance, becoming fainter and fainter with each ridge. After you enjoy this view, it will be time to backtrack down the mountain to Road 23 and continue the southward journey so you can arrive in Trout Lake or the Columbia Gorge before dark.

The drive through the Cascade forest is generally uneventful because the road is so well maintained. An occasional forest service campground has been built along the way, and a cluster of them are just north of the border of the Mount Adams Wilderness Area. These lakes and campgrounds—Olallie Lake, Chain of Lakes, and Takhlakh—have excellent views of Mount Adams and are among the most popular of the car campgrounds in the national forest. You can try for a camping site, but don't be surprised if they're all taken, especially in midsummer.

Occasionally you will see the 12,276-foot Mount Adams through the timber, but you haven't seen a snow-capped volcano until you've rounded the curve near Council Lake and seen Adams looming up above you, looking as benign as a big ice-cream cone. As Northwest volcanoes go, benign is a good description of Mount Adams. It hasn't erupted in recorded history, although it is still classified as active. It is also easy to climb, as 12,000-foot peaks go. Climbing it requires very little technical skill and in good weather isn't much more than a long uphill hike.

Don't use all of your film on the first or even the second great view of the mountain because you'll regret it when the road runs along the edge of a hill with perhaps half a mile of unobstructed Mount Adams views.

The road meanders through the forest and down to level land, and suddenly you are in the small town of Trout Lake, where you can get gas for your car and food for yourself in a cafe at the main intersection. Gifford Pinchot National Forest has a ranger station on the western edge of town. A good place to stay or have dinner is the Mio Amore Pensione just south of town. The owner-chef serves only one dish each night at dinner, and selects it in an interesting fashion: The first person to call for a dinner reservation is given a choice of three entrées. The one selected is what everyone eats that night.

This route continues due east of Trout Lake to Glenwood on an unmarked county road. Or at least it did when I last drove it. The road takes off east from Road 23 about a hundred yards north of Trout Lake and passes several well-tended ranches and hay farms before beginning a slight climb above the valley to cross a low divide. The drive to Glenwood is uneventful as it crosses mainly flatland with a few trees. You'll occasionally see Mount Adams off to the northwest and Mount Hood is across the Columbia River to the south.

Glenwood is a very small town with a cowboy flavor. The dense timber of Gifford Pinchot National Forest has been left behind in the Cascades and the parched landscape is more John Ford western than Paul Bunyan lumberjack because the rainfall has dropped dramatically.

Just east of Glenwood the road reaches the Klickitat River canyon and pine forests that feel more spacious than the quite

A gnarled alpine larch

claustrophobic Cascade forests. The road skirts the edge of the sheer basaltic cliffs and the highway department has built only an occasional turnout so we can enjoy the view of the deep canyon. Eventually the road descends to cross the Klick-itat, then climbs slowly along the northern side of the canyon.

This road gives you great views of the surrounding countryside and an occasional thrill when a logging truck comes barreling down the highway, flinging chunks of bark, gravel, and dust.

The first time I drove this route my arrival coincided with a population explosion in the grasshopper world. So many hit my windshield that it sounded as though someone was hitting the car with handfuls of wheat. Several joined me inside the car before I could roll up the window. I drove through them for perhaps two hundred yards and as suddenly was out of the grasshopper cloud. I stopped to throw out the hitchhikers and scrape the casualties off the grill and windshield. When I arrived in Goldendale I had to use a garden hose to clean the radiator grill.

When the road emerges from the rough hills along the Klickitat, it joins State 142 a short distance from Goldendale.

In the Area

Gifford Pinchot National Forest, 206-750-5000

Mount St. Helens National Volcanic Monument, 206-247-5473

Mount St. Helens Visitor Center, 206-274-6644

Mio Amore Pensione, 509-395-2264

11 ~

The Columbia Gorge Route

This trip follows the north side of the Columbia River upriver from Vancouver via the famed Columbia gorge that cuts through the Cascade Range and into the eastern Washington desert.

Highlights: *Fort Vancouver, towboats and barges, sailboarders, waterfalls, mountain scenery, eccentric art museum, desert topography, and a winery.*

Begin this long trip (about 200 miles) at Fort Vancouver, where the Hudson's Bay Company had its outpost through the middle of the nineteenth century. The Fort Vancouver National Monument is just off I-5, an almost exact replica that shows how the trappers and factors lived when the British and Americans were jockeying for power and territory. This was one of the most important sites in the history of the Pacific Northwest because it was the unofficial goal of many Americans migrating across the plains and mountains to the Oregon Country. Many of them arrived at the post without much more than they were wearing because their route down the

Columbia River was one of the worst: Rafts upset, horses drowned, and goods disappeared beneath the water.

Although he was under orders to discourage Americans from settling in the region, Dr. John McLoughlin, the chief factor of Fort Vancouver, was too kind and generous for the good of Hudson's Bay Company, and he helped the new-comers as much as he could. Eventually he was fired for his humanitarian efforts, and he lived out his life in Oregon City amid Americans. Finally the Americans won the boundary dispute and the English had to withdraw to what is now Canada. Some locals think the Canadians got their revenge by naming their city Vancouver, which grew much larger than the American Vancouver.

Fort Vancouver is almost surrounded by remnants of the Vancouver Barracks, an army post, built later by Americans, that would hardly be known to anyone today were it not for the service of a lowly, lonely lieutenant named Ulysses S. Grant, who served there a few years before the Civil War broke out. Vancouver has an elegance about it, thanks to the row of Vancouver Barracks officers' residences and other Victorian-era buildings, that hasn't been diminished by the heavy commuter traffic between it and Portland. It also has one of the state's more interesting trees growing in a protected area downtown. It is believed to be the first apple tree brought to the Pacific Northwest.

From Vancouver, take State 14 east through Camas and Washougal. Compared with the fast, level I-84 that runs along the river on the Oregon side, State 14 is a country road. It is two-lane and very crooked as it follows the contours of the land rather than slicing through. It is for drivers who have some extra time to spend on the road; those in a hurry will cross into Oregon and zoom down I-84.

Although neither Camas nor Washougal is yet a desti-nation town, you might want to stop in Washougal for a self-guided tour of the Pendleton Woolen Mills factory or visit the Pendleton factory outlet shop, where you can buy clothing at reduced rates.

Just east of Washougal you will enter the 292,000-acre Columbia River Gorge National Scenic Area, created in 1986 to protect the scenic, cultural, recreational, and natural resources of the gorge while encouraging growth only in urban areas. The scenic area created a partnership between the forest service, a commission to oversee the gorge, the tribes, and six local counties. The scenic area takes in both sides of the river for some seventy miles, ending at the Maryhill Museum near US 97 in the desert. As with all programs that limit the uses of private land, the scenic area remains controversial among locals but its popularity continues to grow with visitors.

The first of many places to stop for the scenery is Cape Horn, with a view many miles upriver that will give you an idea of what you will see along the way. Beacon Rock State Park is next and it stands more than 800 feet tall, the largest monolith of its kind in America. It became a state park after it was almost destroyed when the man who owned it wanted to turn it into a vertical rock quarry. You can climb to its summit on steps with handrails, but be warned that it is a long and steep climb.

From the rock you can see Bonneville Dam, the first of the series of dams that changed the Columbia forever. At one time the river had immense falls, a series of cascades, deadly rapids, and whirlpools. All of these were covered by the chain of hydroelectric dams that stretch from Bonneville upstream into Canada. Only one stretch of the Columbia still flows free in Washington, a sixty-mile section that goes through the Hanford nuclear reservation.

Bonneville Dam is where the effect of the tides stops, and where boats and towboats and barges start through a series of locks to make their way upriver. You will see many towboats pushing a group of barges up and down the river, hauling grain to Portland or beyond, taking fuel upriver, and carrying many other kinds of cargo. The towboats and barges have been built especially for the locks and fit them exactly. A load, called a "lockage," on the Columbia is much smaller than those on the Mississippi, where a lockage may be a quarter of a mile long. In contrast, the Columbia River locks limit the lockages to 630 feet long and 84 feet wide.

Barges are the most economical means of moving freight. As an example, to move 3,500 tons of grain downriver, it would take 116 semitrailers or 35 railcars. However, only one towboat and one barge can do the job for sixteen cents per bushel, in 1992 prices, compared with thirty-two cents by rail and ninety-one cents by truck.

Since the dams were built, much of the color of river travel has disappeared. Excitement and danger still exist for boatmen, and the wind, snow, and rain are as uncomfortable as they always were. Before the dams, boatmen had special skills that enabled them to navigate a line of barges on the swift current and among the rocks that, with one bit of poor judgment, could cause the barges to stack up on rocks or sink. Many of the rocks in the river were named for tug skippers who missed a crucial turn in a spectacular fashion.

One of the smallest towns in the state is Skamania, which is mostly a single building that houses the post office, grocery, and general store. It is a good place to stock up on snacks and souvenirs.

Stevenson is the next town, small and unpretentious, with a good county museum. It is the county seat of Skamania County and earned a degree of fame for being the first government to pass a law making it a crime to kill a Sasquatch, or Bigfoot. Although few members of the county council really believed the creature exists, they wanted to take no chances if one should be found.

Stevenson is the first of a cluster of towns, some no more than a building or two, built in the heart of the Cascade Range. Others are Home Valley, Cook, Underwood, White Salmon, and Bingen. Lodging is often difficult to find along here because the few places to stay are so popular, such as Carson Hot Springs, where guests come year after year for the mineral baths and solitude. The Skamania Lodge is a new destination resort here.

From White Salmon eastward the scenery changes rapidly from the damp, evergreen forests of western Washington to the dry, open country of eastern Washington. The geology becomes more stark and dramatic as old lava flows appear in the form of basaltic cliffs and outcroppings. From here eastward basalt in all its shapes, sizes, and colors dominates the landscape.

Two north-south highways join State 14 along here: Forest Service Road 30 comes down the Wind River from the Gifford Pinchot National Forest and the southern flank of Mount St. Helens, and State 141 comes down from Trout Lake and Mount Adams. An interesting alternate trip is to take State 141 north to Trout Lake, then follow the paved county road east to the cowboy town of Glenwood and back down to the Columbia River on State 142.

Continuing eastward on State 14, you may want to stop in Bingen for a meal and a tour of the Mont Elise Winery in the middle of town. It is the largest of five or six wineries in the gorge and the most popular wine they produce is gewürztraminer.

After Bingen you are in open country, extremely hot in the summer and extremely cold in the winter. You'll already

Windsurfer on the Columbia

have noted the strong wind that blows almost constantly
through the gorge, sort of an enormous regional breathing as
the air rushes back and forth through the Cascades, depending on the pressure systems on either side of the mountains.
The gorge is one of the best places in the world for wind-
surfing, and world championship competitions are held here

each year. Since the water and air are so cold, nearly every windsurfer wears a wet or dry suit while they dart like water bugs among the towboat and barge traffic.

Keep an eye out for the Maryhill Museum just before the intersection with US 97, the major north-south highway that runs from Canada to California. Maryhill Museum is one of the nation's most eccentric museums, and one of the best in the Northwest, in spite of its remote location.

It began as a desert palace for a multimillionaire named Samuel Hill (Yes, the expression "What in Sam Hill!" came from him). He married Mary Hill, daughter of the railroad magnate James J. Hill, and she didn't have to go to the bother of learning a new surname. Sam Hill bought about 7,000 acres of land for his castle and tried to lure a group of Quakers to start a colony there. The Quakers didn't bite. Neither did his wife, Mary, in spite of his naming the place in her honor: Apparently she never even visited it. After living in Seattle a few years, she returned to the Midwest and lived apart from her energetic husband.

Hill made himself a moving target during his full life. He conceived of the Peace Arch at the U.S.–Canadian border at Blaine and got schoolchildren involved in the fund raising and construction. He was largely responsible for construction of the beautiful old Columbia Gorge Highway on the Oregon side, which is being restored: He even underwrote it with his own money.

After World War I, President Wilson appointed Hill to a commission to help rebuild Europe, and it was then that he met two women who became important in his life. The first was an American dancer named Loie Fuller, who introduced him around Paris, even to the sculptor Auguste Rodin. He also befriended Queen Marie of Romania.

After numerous mishaps and failed opportunities, Hill decided to turn his sagebrush palace into a museum and

Queen Marie of Romania came to dedicate it in 1926. Hill died before the museum could be completed, but another wealthy friend, Anna Spreckles of the sugar dynasty, took over and completed the place. It has been open ever since and is supported in part by leases on the estate surrounding it. The museum houses a major collection of Rodin sculpture, many articles donated by Queen Marie, and a major collection of regional Indian artifacts.

Just after State 14 crosses US 97, you will see a sign warning you that you won't find gasoline or food for eighty miles. This stretch is obviously very lonely, but it is a good highway and the scenery is open, with outcroppings of basalt lining the two-lane blacktop and river. The route is hilly in places, but the drive is fast because traffic is almost always light. At the end of the eighty miles State 14 runs into I-82 at Plymouth. High on the windswept hill above the river and near the intersection is the Columbia Crest Winery, the largest in eastern Washington and part of the Ste. Michelle company. The winery has a visitors' area where you can watch part of the winemaking process, and a large gift shop where you can buy wine, picnic supplies, and gifts.

From here you can take a sharp turn north on I-82 through the Horse Heaven Hills twenty-four miles to Kennewick or turn south and cross the river into Oregon.

In the Area

Fort Vancouver National Monument, 206-696-7655

Pendleton Woolen Mills Outlet, 206-835-2131

Columbia River Gorge National Scenic Area, 503-386-2333

Mont Elise Winery, 509-493-3000

Maryhill Museum, 509-773-3733

Columbia Crest Winery, 509-875-2061

12 ~

Bickleton:
Bluebirds in Horse Heaven

From State 22 southeast of Yakima: Take the Bickleton-Goldendale Road south through the Horse Heaven Hills to US 97 at Goldendale.

Highlights: *Open, windy country with almost no sign of people, biggest collection of occupied bluebird houses in the Northwest, if not the West Coast.*

If you've taken in too much liquid in the form of the award-winning Yakima Valley wines and the wonderful fruits and vegetables sold at roadside stands everywhere, this route down to the Columbia River is a good way to dry out.

The Mabton-Goldendale road is a classic two-lane blacktop and, like most such roads in Washington, it is reasonably well maintained. That means your suspension system should be none the worse for wear when you return to a major highway. The road isn't too well marked in Mabton, but if you get confused or totally lost, stop at any roadside stand or service station and ask directions. This is also a good place to brush up on your Spanish because a large percentage of the Yakima Valley population is first- or second-generation Hispanic.

Once the road takes you out of the valley and onto the high plains, you will quickly learn that lonesome roads do exist. An occasional ranch house appears, and irrigation is making inroads into the area for row crops and vineyards, but for the most part it is a seldom-traveled road. In the occasional draw, or shallow canyon, you'll see oak trees that have managed to survive on the meager water supply, and most creek beds you see will be as barren as the land around them.

After driving several miles, you will see the town of Bickleton off in the distance, and not long before you arrive you will see the first of the bluebird houses perched on fence posts or their own tall poles. As you enter town you'll see the tidy

Horse Heaven

little houses everywhere, in gardens, on the sides of buildings, and atop homes. In front of the community church sits a bluebird house that is a tiny replica of the church.

All of this is because many years ago a Bickleton couple began building the houses as a hobby and because bluebirds were their favorite of the birds that migrated in and out of the area. Each spring they took down the little houses for cleaning and had them back up in time for the bluebirds to arrive. Soon other residents took up the hobby, and after the originators died the tradition continued without change.

Bickleton is a tiny town with some buildings in a western theme and a few Victorian homes, including one rather grand one that was almost in ruins when I last drove through. It has a grocery store, a tavern, a post office, and a cafe that is the town gathering place. The cafe has a collection of large family-size tables, similar to the conference tables hotels provide for meetings, and smaller tables for couples or individuals. It is one of the most casual, and friendly, places you'll find anywhere in the state.

Bickleton has kept its own schools—it is almost too far from the Yakima Valley or Goldendale for school busing—but in 1992 only one student was in the high school graduating class.

As you drive out of town you'll continue seeing bluebird houses on fence posts, and after you've gone perhaps a mile south, you'll have one of the best views of Bickleton. From here it looks something like the set of an early Clint Eastwood film.

Cleveland is the next town, but little is left other than an enormous cemetery and a small cluster of homes.

Not far south of Cleveland you'll begin getting views of Mount Hood in Oregon, assuming you have clear weather, and Mount Adams in Washington. The landscape becomes more broken, with jumbled basalt outcroppings and boulders, and sudden canyons. The road becomes more crooked and slower, and one stretch, down to Rock Creek and through Badger Gulch, was still unpaved when I last drove through.

The population increases as you near Goldendale, and water from deep wells has turned some of the desert into prosperous farms where you'll see row crops, lush grain, and an occasional sunflower farm. I had always assumed sunflowers keep their faces to the sun like teenage girls on the beach. Those I saw near Goldendale were still looking east although the sun was low in the west. Are sunflowers as stupid as turkeys that hold their heads up in rainstorms and drown? Or is that a folktale, too?

In the Area

East Klickitat Chamber of Commerce, 509-374-5301

13 ~

The Snake River Canyon

From Clarkston: Cross the Snake River and take US 12 north from Lewiston to Front Street and follow the signs to Wilma that will bring you back into Washington. Stay on the same road all the way to Pullman.

Highlights: *Some of Washington's Snake River canyon topography, orchards, and typical Palouse country landscapes.*

I happened on to this trip in the best of all possible ways: I saw the road marked on a map and took my chances because I had seen several sections of the Snake River in Washington, but hadn't been able to follow it any distance. This country-roads roulette procedure doesn't always work so well. I've found myself dead-ended in barnyards and on roads much too rough for a sedan. But this one was just fine.

All of the Snake River you'll see on this trip is slack water due to the series of dams that have turned the swift and treacherous river into calm water. It doesn't take a soaring imagination to get an idea of what the river was like before the dams. After reading accounts of travel on the river in those early days, it seems miraculous that anyone survived a trip on it.

The first accounts were those of Lewis and Clark, and the members of their party who kept their own journals. The twenty-eight-member party had almost frozen and starved to death while crossing the Bitterroot Mountains from the Missouri River headwaters into the Columbia River system via the Clearwater River. When they finally arrived on the lower Clearwater, which empties into the Snake at Lewiston, the local Nez Perce gave them food, mostly dried salmon, which made some of the men extremely ill. Lewis and Clark urged the men on so they could get to the Pacific Ocean before the worst of winter arrived. Men who were very ill with abdominal cramps and the attendant inconvenience worked with the healthy to build canoes for the Snake and Columbia trip.

When they launched their armada of unstable canoes, some of the men were too ill to do anything other than lie in the bottoms of the canoes, some of which swamped in the Snake. Nobody drowned, although some came close. Neither Lewis nor Clark was impressed with the scenery they were going through: It just meant a lot of work and discomfort to them.

That was the assessment of many early settlers, and when the steamboats began working the Snake, the toll in human lives, boats, barges, and freight was enormous. The major cargo was grain from the rich fields of the Palouse country. Even with the problems, shipping by boat and barge was much cheaper than by rail. It still is, which is why you'll see so many barges along the river.

Like Lewis and Clark, the pioneer shippers and growers weren't thrilled by the river scenery. The more beautiful it

Washington is known for its apples

was, the more it cost them. This canyon scenery also made it just plain difficult to get the grain aboard the barges. Only a few places were flat enough to permit the horse-drawn wagons of grain to come right to the river's edge. With most of the river's course through the best wheat-growing area running down in deep, steep canyons, the growers and shippers tried transporting the grain from the roads above to the river below by means of chutes. This didn't work well because the friction ground the grain into flour or meal. Much of what arrived at the bottom was wheat dust. New chutes were built that controlled the speed of the grain, but nothing worked as well as it should have. Finally trucks came onto the scene, which made it more practical to haul the grain longer distances to a decent landing.

Today only an occasional board or groove in the canyon walls reminds us of the chutes. Enormous storage tanks and elevators store the grain until it can be transported downriver.

When the settlers began filling the higher ground, others were forced to try the river bottom. They found small protected areas that we now call microclimates in the canyons. Some of these were perfect for growing fruit. So many orchards grew in the area that it became a tradition for people from all over the area to go down to the orchards to pick their own fruit. Unfortunately, many of the original orchards were victims of the flooding behind the dams.

During all of those pioneer years steamboats were the only form of transportation in the Snake canyon, but in 1908 a railroad was opened between Riparia and Lewiston. Before long a rough road was built along the tracks for horse-drawn vehicles, then automobiles.

The canyon is really tame now—you'll find no white water and its roads are even better than before. When the Lower Granite Dam's floodgates closed in 1974, it flooded the canyon here to a depth of eighty feet. The Army Corps of Engineers had to build new roadbeds for both the highway and railroad. Unfortunately, on the first part of this trip the railroad is between the highway and the river, but later on the paved highway and railroad switch sides and several turnouts were built so you can stop and watch the towboats bringing the barges around the innumerable twists and turns of the canyon.

The road suddenly takes a sharp right turn and heads north through a V-shaped canyon and soon emerges on the wheat plateau. If you stay on the same road, it will take you into Pullman.

In the Area

Clarkston Chamber of Commerce, 509-758-7712

14 ~

The Best

of the

Palouse

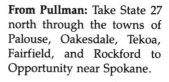

From Pullman: Take State 27 north through the towns of Palouse, Oakesdale, Tekoa, Fairfield, and Rockford to Opportunity near Spokane.

Highlights: *The heart of the famed Palouse country, some of the richest wheat-growing land in the world, plus some small farming towns and Steptoe Butte.*

Although it is a word that describes a geographic area as well as an abbreviation for the popular saddle horse called Appaloosa, the origins of *Palouse* is something of a mystery. Nobody knows exactly what it meant in the language of the Native Americans, from whom the whites borrowed the word. They called themselves Palouse, or something similar, but didn't know why, nor did they know what the word meant.

Today the name means some of the most productive farming land in the world, and to those of us who like open landscapes, it means one of the most beautiful parts of the Northwest.

The Palouse country has no distinct boundaries, but in general it runs north from the Snake River to the Spokane River valley, west into the channeled scablands, which are bordered (more or less) on the west by I-90, and the eastern boundary is where the timber begins in western Idaho. The landscape is notable for its deep soil, which is *loess*, meaning it has been blown in by the wind that comes out of the southwest every day, steady and dependable as a river. The soil is more than 100 feet deep in some places.

Most of the Palouse is low but steep, rolling hills with an elevation that ranges from about 1,200 feet to a little more than 2,000 feet. This altitude gain is crucial to the Palouse because the elevation catches the rainfall that skips over the area from the Cascade Range to the Palouse, which includes the Columbia Basin and the dryland wheat-farming area west of the channeled scablands.

This elevation gain is impossible to detect as you drive east, but it shows up dramatically in the wheat production figures. The Palouse gets thirty bushels or more per acre than wheat farms less than twenty miles away. As with all agriculture, it is the amount of water that makes the difference. A great advantage the Palouse farmers have over their Great Plains counterparts is the almost total absence of crop loss to weather. A few years ago the head of the cooperative extension service in Pullman told me that the Palouse farmers had never had a crop failure. "Never!" he emphasized.

When the first combines were built to thresh wheat, the steep hills of the Palouse created major problems. The body of the combine, called the separator because it is where the grain is separated from the stalks and chaff, must be kept level in order to work properly. The earliest mobile combines' separators were kept level by turning large wheels on ratchets to raise and lower each side. In the Palouse this meant a lot of

Rich wheat-growing country in the Palouse

work. Then when the self-propelled combines arrived that were operated by only one person, they were good only on flatland, such as the Great Plains.

Enter a man from the Palouse named Hansen. Some of his neighbors called him "Haywire" Hansen because he was always building things, inventing easier ways to do things. It wasn't long before Hansen had a solution to the combine leveling problem. He invented a motorized ratchet system that kicked on and off by a mercury switch. When the combine tilted, the mercury slid down to trip the switch, which started a motor or hydraulic pump that raised or lowered one side of the combine until it was level. Then the mercury returned to the middle of the switch, much like the bubble in a leveling device, breaking electrical contact to shut off the level.

91

My favorite time to take a trip through these steep Palouse Hills is in the spring when everything is green, and the best time of day is early or late when the shadows sharply define the landscape. My favorite drive is on US 27, which begins in Pullman and ends in the Spokane River valley at Opportunity. It is a slow and crooked highway lined with mailboxes and farmhouses, and you'll share it with tractors pulling various farm equipment from field to field and farmers who often drive slowly so they can look at their crops and check fences.

A short distance out of Pullman you'll come to the turn to Kamiak Butte State Park, featuring a 3,360-foot peak that stands high above the rolling hills. It was named for a Yakima chief named Kamiakin, a notable warrior who defeated the U.S. Army from time to time.

The first town out of Pullman is Palouse, on the banks of the river of the same name. The town has lots of brick buildings, and although the great old hardware store finally closed and sold off its fixtures to a local collector, most of Palouse's small-town charm remains. Palouse is close enough to the college crowd at Pullman and the gentry of Spokane to have a deli with specialty coffee.

As you drive along this road, and several other more modest two-lane blacktop roads, you'll notice that although the road may have been perfectly straight as it went across the farmlands, just before it enters a town it makes one, sometimes two, sudden sharp turns. This was planned. It was an effort by highway engineers to force drivers to slow down before entering towns.

Just north of Palouse in Garfield is a county road leading off to the west marked "Elberton." It is worth an hour's delay to drive over to visit the remnants of this once-thriving town. It can't accurately be called a ghost town because people still live there, but most of the businesses and churches have been removed. Several years ago the county government planned to turn the remnants of the town into a working museum with the post office still functioning, along with the general store. But funds weren't forthcoming and the town, which once was an important milling center, became mostly a memory. Elberton was beautifully sited on the Palouse River with ancient trees lining the street and riverbank.

Another good side trip is from Oakesdale to Steptoe Butte State Park. As parks go, it's small—just a picnic table or two at the foot of the peak, but the peak itself is much more impressive. It rises 3,600 feet above the Palouse Hills and its summit is reached by a road that corkscrews around and around until it reaches the summit, which bristles with radio and television transmission towers.

Steptoe was named for Colonel Edward J. Steptoe, who in 1858 was soundly defeated by Native Americans. Steptoe wasn't even properly armed for the battle; his supply crew had left most of the weapons and ammunition behind when they struck out from Walla Walla. Fortunately, Steptoe was a better tactician than quartermaster and managed to escape in the dead of night with nearly all of his men. They made a forced march across the Palouse Hills toward Walla Walla and were not pursued by the warriors.

Steptoe Butte was later purchased by one of those extremely self-confident Englishmen who appeared frequently on the frontier. James Davis and his family were searching for a new home in a wagon he bought in Walla Walla. After several stops that brought the opinion from Davis that the places were "not quite right," his wife finally had had enough when they came to a pretty grove of trees with a stream flowing through. She announced she wasn't going a foot farther, so there they stopped and founded the town of Cottonwood Springs. It was renamed Cashup in honor of

Davis, who earned the nickname from his method of running a general store: "Cash up front," he insisted to one and all.

Davis owned the nearby butte, then called Pyramid Peak, and atop it he built a magnificent hotel with a wraparound balcony and decorated it with locally grown wheat and furniture imported from England and the East Coast of America. The hotel was accidentally burned in 1911, after standing idle since Davis's death in 1896.

Eventually the peak was renamed Steptoe Butte, and then a geologist made an interesting discovery: He found that the butte was actually the tip of a granite mountain protruding above the lava flows that covered the rest of the range. The word *steptoe* entered the language of geology and refers to any similar protrusion of an older formation above newer materials.

From Oakesdale the road follows the line of least resistance to the pleasant town of Tekoa, virtually on the Idaho state line. The road continues on north to Fairfield, and when you arrive here you are effectively out of the Palouse country and into the Spokane region. The difference is rainfall and topography. Here rainfall amounts are higher than in the Palouse country, and this leads to slightly different farming methods— more rainfall means more weeds and at the same time greater crop yield. Lawn grass seed is a popular crop here. You'll also note that the timber is much thicker and more prevalent than in the Palouse.

The route ends when you reach I-90 in Opportunity.

In the Area

All phone numbers are in area code 509.

Pullman Chamber of Commerce, 334-3565

Palouse Chamber of Commerce, 878-1269

15 ~

Crab Creek Valley

From the east side of I-90 bridge at Vantage: Turn south on State 26 to State 243. Follow it to Beverly and take the Crab Creek Valley Road east to State 26.

Highlights: *Ginkgo State Park in Vantage, Wanapum Dam, fish ladder and museum; Crab Creek valley and Saddle Mountains.*

Crab Creek is one of the longest streams in Washington. It begins just west of Spokane and meanders west across the wheat country to Odessa, then gets involved with the Columbia Basin Project as one of the streams that helps drain the water that has been used for irrigation. It heads south, more or less, from the Soap Lake area, enters Moses Lake and temporarily loses itself in the lake, then reemerges below the Potholes Reservoir with its own identity again. Soon it heads due west along the base of the Saddle Mountains and finally enters the Columbia River just downstream from the very small town of Beverly.

Some geography students like to follow the creek from its source to the Columbia, but that is too complicated for me. My favorite part is the last stretch between Othello and the Columbia, where the creek wanders along the base of the mountains and is paralleled by a modest road.

Taking this road is a good excuse to stop at the Ginkgo State Park at Vantage. Be warned: If you visit Vantage in July or August, you might as well be in Twentynine Palms, California, because the temperature can soar to more than 110 degrees Fahrenheit down in the Columbia River canyon. However, the state park is worth the sunburn because it has the best collection of petrified wood in the state: More than 200 species of petrified wood have been identified, including the ginkgo, which is now extinct in America.

From Vantage, go east across the Columbia River and turn south immediately after crossing the bridge. Take State 26 until the intersection with the more modest State 243. Take it south along the river to Beverly.

It was at this intersection that my son and I once had a strange adventure. We were coming up from Beverly and were waiting at the State 243–State 26 junction for trucks to pass when a semi loaded with hay came roaring down the hill. When it turned south on the sharp curve there, a whole section of baled hay flew off and scattered along the road like scraps of paper.

I parked and my son and I ran over to pull the hay off the road before someone hit it with a car. Another car stopped and the driver got out to help, and another truck loaded with hay stopped. He radioed ahead to tell the trucker he had lost part of his load.

Only after we had dragged several bales off the highway did I see a man sitting on a bale in the ditch, holding his head. I said what everyone says in such a situation: "Are you all right?"

He didn't answer for a moment. He was covered with hay and dirt and his right hand was skinned. He didn't have any teeth, and he hadn't shaved in a few days.

"I think so," he finally said. "I'll be all right in a minute."

Then he started talking and was still talking when we drove away several minutes later.

"I was just walking along when he dumped his load on me," he said. Neither my son nor I saw him beside the road when we were waiting for traffic to clear.

"Knocked my feet right out from under me. My cigarette lighter is laying way over there," he said, pointing toward the ditch. My son, the truck driver, and I stopped working and stood around listening to his story. "I was just walking along when, boom! he got me. I ran out of gas up at Moses Lake and was walking down here where I've got a cache of gas behind a pile of rocks."

Then he lost all of us. Moses Lake is about forty miles away, on another highway, and none of us believed him. He

A barn in eastern Washington

kept talking, elaborating his story and trying to sound put-upon for being such an innocent victim. We decided that he had hidden between the stacks of baled hay to hitch a ride, but had loosened them so much that they flew off on the first turn. He was still talking when we left. I have always wondered if the gods of circumstance weren't feeling a little petulant that day.

Although I'm personally not fond of dams even though I am using electricity from them at this very moment, you may want to stop at the Wanapum Dam because it has a good regional museum that emphasizes Native American culture, and a viewing window where you can watch salmon and other fish using the ladder around the dam.

The Crab Creek route begins in Beverly, a small sun-baked town overlooking the Columbia. It is worth noting that the Columbia from Wanapum Dam downriver through the Hanford nuclear reservation is the only stretch of the river in the United States that still flows uninhibited by dams. It isn't a long stretch—only about sixty miles—and its volume is controlled by the dams upstream. At least the water moves, giving you a sense of what it was before the arrival of dams and the hydroelectric aluminum plants the dams brought to the banks of the river. The dams and aluminum plants were built in the days before power brokers even thought of comparing the number of jobs created with the cost to the fishing industry and the Native American culture.

All along the lower Crab Creek valley Saddle Mountain looms over the eastern bank, casting long shadows in the morning and showing various colors in the evening. Some of the mountain is smooth and looks as though you could hike to the top in an hour or so. In other places it is a sheer cliff with wind-carved hoodoos creating almost as many forms as a summer cloud. The valley is particularly pretty in the spring, when all plants are green and desert wildflowers bloom on the valley floor and up the sides of Saddle Mountain.

Part of the valley's extensive sand dunes have been designated a playground for all-terrain vehicles. The rest of the valley is divided among farming, grazing, the wetlands of the Crab Creek Wildlife Area, and parts of the Columbia National Wildlife Refuge. Here you'll see birds among the marsh grass year-round ranging from migratory waterfowl to small songbirds. Small lakes spot the valley. Some of the lakes have bans on motors, and fishermen must hike in with their equipment. Since Crab Creek is part of the Columbia basin's drainage system, its water is rich with nutrients and the rainbow and eastern brook trout grow to larger than usual sizes.

Most of the road through the valley is dirt and gravel, the kind that forces you to drive slower than usual so you can savor the quiet beauty of the place. You will go through the remnants of two towns that thrived briefly in the valley. The valley was settled when the Milwaukee Railroad was built long after the major railroads reached the West Coast. The Milwaukee line didn't have the advantage of free land that was given to the other railroads—like Great Northern and Union Pacific—and it had to buy track right of way in more hostile and less populated areas. In the Crab Creek valley at least three sidings were built—Smyrna, Corfu, and Taunton. Today only a suggestion remains of each. The last time I drove through the valley, the schoolhouse in Smyrna had been converted into a home.

The Milwaukee Railroad went out of business several years ago and the state of Washington acquired the track bed for use as a cross-state hiking, horseback, and bicycle trail, parts of which were named in honor of the patriotic actor, John Wayne.

The route ends when the road intersects with State 26 a few miles west of Othello.

In the Area

All phone numbers are in area code 509.

Gingko Petrified Forest State Park, 856-2700
Columbia National Wildlife Refuge, 488-2668
Columbia Basin Wildlife Area, 765-6641

16 ~

Moses Coulee

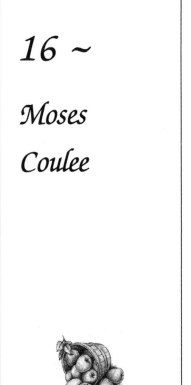

From East Wenatchee: Take State 28 south from East Wenatchee along the Columbia River and watch for the Appledale-Palisades turn to the northeast. Follow this road all the way to US 2.

Highlights: *A classic example of the coulees formed during the Ice Age when the course of the Columbia River was changed by ice and debris dams.*

Until I came to Washington I had never heard of a coulee. The first time I heard the word in Washtucna I thought the farmers were talking about Chinese laborers brought to America to build the railroads. No, they were talking about the dry canyons that dot the landscape of eastern Washington. They were created by a series of enormous floods and by ice and debris dams that changed the course of the Columbia River during the Ice Age.

I have no idea how many are on maps, but they are all through the channeled scablands and over in the Big Bend area, where the Columbia flowed in a different channel when the river was dammed and forced westward, where it created the Dry Falls, now a state park.

The channeled scablands are the broken country you'll see on the western edge of the Palouse country. The scablands begin around Spokane and fan out and converge again at the Columbia gorge. They consist of numerous coulees and hundreds of ship rocks, those lonely sentinels that stand erect over the rugged landscape. Nearly all of these ship rocks are on a northeast-southwest axis, and they are distinguished by sharp prows that face the northeast and more blunt southwest points. Many don't really have a southwest end; they just dwindle off into the landscape.

All geologists were taught that all things related to their profession were the result of gradual forces, the buildup by lava, by uplifting and other equally slow processes, and that these things were broken down at equally slow paces, mostly by wind and water.

A geologist named Harlan Bretz, who taught at the University of Chicago, had a different idea that came to him while flying over the channeled scablands. He had never been comfortable with the belief that water erosion had created the area over thousands or millions of years. In most cases, some water still flowed in these areas, and in the channeled scablands none flowed and there were no signs that any streams had ever flowed there. What if the scablands were created by a single catastrophic flood, he asked himself, or maybe a series of catastrophic floods? He began accumulating information and evidence. By tracing the direction of the ship rocks and the chain of small lakes that had formed south of Spokane, he found that the source of the water that caused the enormous erosion lay east of Spokane.

He kept following the signs east into Montana and came at last to the source. On the mountains surrounding the Missoula basin, he found what he was convinced were water marks high on the mountains. He was sure he had found the source, and soon he had the cause. He believed that ice and dirt dams had turned the basin into a gigantic lake. When the ice melted, the water formed a wall several hundred feet high and it rushed eastward across the Idaho Panhandle, on to the Spokane valley, and there the lay of the land forced the water southwest across the low hills. The flood of biblical proportions washed away the topsoil and took with it billions of tons of soil and rocks. When it hit the Columbia gorge, the Cascade Mountains in Oregon at last turned the flood and channeled it down the Columbia River and eventually out to sea.

Bretz's theory was flexible enough to support the possibility of a series of such catastrophic floods. It took him years to get support from the geological community, but eventually it came around and today hardly anyone doubts that Bretz stumbled onto one of the great happenings in geologic history.

A drive up Moses Coulee won't be nearly as dramatic, but it is a pleasant drive and makes a good alternative when you're driving across the state on the transcontinental US 2. Start by taking State 28 south from East Wenachee along the Columbia River past the Rock Island Dam and an aluminum plant. Take the Appledale-Palisades turn to the northeast. It is a narrow but paved road and was in good condition the two times I drove through.

Moses Coulee was named for a popular Native American chief in the area. He was so well liked, in fact, that the settlers also gave his name to a small lake some distance south, where his band lived part of the time. Moses Lake grew into one of the major towns of the area.

The floor of the coulee is as flat as a table and irrigated fields alternate with miles of sagebrush. Occasionally the road swings over close to one of the coulee walls, where you can see crumbling basalt that adds more and more debris around the base of the walls. One section of the wall is pocked as though it has been attacked by a demented woodpecker.

When driving country roads you never know what to expect from towns that appear on maps. More and more of the smaller ones do not have services at all. Increasingly residents must drive to the nearest town for everything. Appledale and Palisades are no exceptions. They're only collections of modest homes closer together than usual.

After about seventeen miles the blacktop gives way to a gravel road that swings over against the east wall, past irrigation sprinklers, and rather suddenly right into the front yard of a ranch house. My first thought was that I had done it again; missed a turn and here I was in somebody's backyard and they'd undoubtedly have a big dog that liked to eat car fenders. Then I saw that the road took a sharp right turn and headed up a steep grade. I took it, and soon I was on a level bench, then climbing again along the face of the coulee wall on a road blasted out of the basalt. Then suddenly there I was, out of the coulee and on a level gravel road between wheat fields. Well!

I came to a T-intersection and took the left road back toward the coulee and soon I was back in the coulee again. In a very short time I was on a road along the top of the low wall on the west side of the coulee and below me was an irrigation system that I'd heard of for years. I knew farmers who drove a hundred miles just to see how that system worked.

Here the coulee walls narrowed and the land between them was flat and the soil rich. The owner strung cables back and forth across between the walls, high enough to clear all his farm equipment. From these cables he hung irrigation pipes and sprinklers and left them always in place. Unlike other farmers, he never had to move the pipes, or take them out of the field when he needed to plant, cultivate, or harvest.

As far as I know, the cables and sprinklers still hang there.

US 2 is only a short distance from this ingenious system.

Bibliography

Blankenship, Russell. *And There Were Men.* New York: Knopf, 1942.

Cantwell, Robert. *The Hidden Northwest.* New York: Lippincott, 1972.

Cook, Warren L. *Flood Tide of Empire: Spain and the Pacific Northwest 1543–1819.* New Haven: Yale University Press, 1973.

Darvill, Fred T. *North Cascades Highway Guide.* Seattle: Pacific Northwest National Parks and Forests Association, 1986.

Hitchman, Robert. *Place Names of Washington.* Tacoma: Washington State Historical Society, 1985.

Holbrook, Stewart. *The Columbia.* New York: Rinehart, 1956.

Meany, Edmond S. *Origin of Washington Place Names.* Seattle: University of Washington Press, 1923.

Meinig, D. W. *The Great Columbia Plain: A Historical Geography 1805–1910.* Seattle: University of Washington Press, 1968.

Mills, Randall V. *Stern-wheelers Up Columbia: A Century of Steamboating in the Oregon Country.* Palo Alto: Pacific Books, 1947.

Morgan, Murray. *The Dam.* New York: Viking, 1954.

———. *The Last Wilderness.* Seattle: University of Washington Press, 1955.

Rowsome, Frank Jr. *The Verse by the Side of the Road.* Brattleboro, Vermont: Stephen Greene Press, 1965.

Speidel, Bill. *The Wet Side of the Mountains.* Seattle: Nettle Creek, 1974.

Weis, Norman D. *Ghost Towns of the Pacific Northwest.* Caldwell, Idaho: Caxton Printers, 1971.

Winthrop, Theodore. *The Canoe and the Saddle.* 1863. Boston: Ticknor and Fields.

Works Progress Administration. *Washington: A Guide to the Evergreen State.* 1940. Portland: Binfords & Mort, 1951.

Index

BRIDGES, DAMS, FERRIES and
  LOCKS
  Bonneville Dam, 59, 74–75
  Columbia River dams, 28, 74–75
  Grays River covered bridge, 63
  Lower Granite Dam, 87
  M/V Coho, Port Angeles, 50
  Port Townsend to Keystone, 21
  Puget Island to Oregon, 62
  Rock Island Dam, East
    Wenachee, 103
  Skagit River dams, 23
  Wanapum Dam, 98

CAVES, COULEES, FOSSILS and
  SHIP ROCKS
  Big Four Inn caves, Silverton, 17
  Moses Coulee, 101–104
  Stonerose fossil bed, Republic,
    27
CITIES and TOWNS
  Aberdeen, 45
  Altoona, 63–64
  Appledale, 104
  Arlington, 9
  Belfair, 37
  Beverly, 95, 96
  Bickleton, 81–82
  Bingen, 76
  Boistfort, 56
  Camas, 73
  Cashup, 93–94
  Cathlamet, 60–62
  Chehalis, 52
  Chesaw, 34
  Chinook, 41–42

Clear Lake, 9
Cleveland, 82
Conconully, 30–31
Concrete, 23
Conttardi, 63–64
Conway, 3–4
Corfu, 99
Cosmopolis, 45
Cottonwood Springs. See
  Cashup
Coupeville, 22
Darrington, 17, 18
Dewatto, 38
Edison, 6
Elberton, 92–93
Everett, 17
Fairfield, 94
Fairhaven, 7
Forks, 48
Frankfort, 64
Glenwood, 69
Goldendale, 83
Granite Falls, 15
Grays River, 63
Holly, 39
Hoquiam, 45
Ilwaco, 42–43
Kettle Falls, 27–28
Keystone, 21–22
La Conner, 4–5
La Push, 48–49
Lebam, 57
Loomis, 31–32
Marblemount, 23–24
Mazama, 24
Moclips, 45

CITIES and TOWNS (*cont.*)
Molson, 33–34
Monte Cristo, 16–17
Moses Lake, 103
Napavine, 52–53
Naselle, 64
Nighthawk, 31, 32
Ocean Shores, 45
Okanogan, 16
Omak, 26
Oroville, 32
Oysterville, 45
Palisades, 104
Palouse, 92
Pe Ell, 56
Pierre. See Pe Ell
Pillar Rock, 63–64
Port Angeles, 50
Port Townsend, 19–21
Queets, 46
Raymond, 45
Republic, 27
Rosburg, 63
Ryderwood, 55
Sappho, 49
Sedro Woolley, 11, 22
Sequim, 50
Shelton, 50
Silverton, 17
Skamania, 75
Skamokawa, 62
Smyrna, 99
Stanwood, 3
Stevenson, 75–76
Sumas, 11–12
Tahuya, 38
Taunton, 99
Tekoa, 94
Tiger, 28
Trout Lake, 69
Tulalip, 2
Twisp, 25
Vancouver, 72–73
Vantage, 96
Warm Beach, 2–3

Washougal, 73–74
Wauconda, 26–27
Westport, 45
White Salmon, 76
Winlock, 53
Winthrop, 24–25
COULEES. See CAVES,
    COULEES, FOSSILS and
    SHIP ROCKS
CREEKS, FALLS, LAKES, RIVERS
    and SPRINGS
Carson Hot Springs, 76
Columbia River, 59–60
Crab Creek, 95–96
Lake Crescent, 49
Marymeer Falls, 49
Skagit River, 3
Snake River, 84–85

DAMS. See BRIDGES, DAMS,
    FERRIES and LOCKS

FALLS. See CREEKS, FALLS,
    LAKES, RIVERS and
    SPRINGS
FARMS and FARMERS'
    MARKETS
Christmas tree farms, Shelton,
    50–51
Conway, 3–4
Darigold cooperative,
    Marysville, 2–3
Oyster farm, Bow, 7
West Shore Acres, La Conner, 5
FERRIES. See BRIDGES, DAMS,
    FERRIES and LOCKS
FESTIVALS
Bluegrass festival, Darrington, 18
FISHING
Bogachiel River, 48
Columbia River, 41–42, 60
Granite Falls Fishway, 15
Pend Oreille River, 28
Lake Quinault, 46
Sauk River, 18

Skagit River, 22–23
Stillaguamish River, 15–16
FORESTS, PARKS and WILDLIFE
Beacon Rock State Park, 74
Belfair State Park, Belfair, 37
Bluebird houses, Bickleton,
    81–82
Bogachiel River State Park, 48
Columbia National Wildlife
    Refuge, 99
Columbia River Gorge National
    Scenic Area, 74
Conconully State Park,
    Conconully, 31
Crab Creek Wildlife Area, 99
Deception Pass State Park, Oak
    Harbor, 22
Fort Canby State Park, Ilwaco,
    42
Fort Casey State Park,
    Keystone, 21–22
Fort Columbia, 41
Ginkgo State Park, Vantage, 96
Julia Butler Hansen National
    Wildlife Refuge, Cathlamet,
    62
Hoh Rain Forest, 46, 47
Kamiak Butte State Park,
    Pullman, 92
Kayak Point County Park,
    Tulalip, 2
Willie Keil's Grave State Park,
    57–58
Larrabee State Park, Fairhaven, 7
Mount Baker-Snoqualmie
    National Forest, Granite Falls,
    15
North Cascades National Park,
    Sedro Woolley, 11, 22, 23–24
Olympic National Park, 46–47,
    49, 50
Padilla Bay state park, Bayview,
    6
Gifford Pinchot National Forest,
    Trout Lake, 69

Quillayute Needles National
    Wildlife Refuge, La Push, 49
Skagit River, 22–23
Steptoe Butte State Park,
    Oakesdale, 93, 94
Tiger, 28
Washington Islands Wilderness
    Area, La Push, 49
FOSSILS. See CAVES, COULEES,
    FOSSILS and SHIP ROCKS

GALLERIES, MUSEUMS,
    SCHOOLS and THEATERS
Fort Worden performing arts
    center, Port Townsend, 21
Historical museum, Republic, 27
Maryhill Museum, 74, 78–79
North Cascades National Park,
    Sedro Woolley, 11
Old Molson museum, Molson, 34
U.S. Coast Guard's National
    Motor Lifeboat School, Cape
    Disappoint, 42–43
Valley Museum of Northwest
    Art, La Conner, 5
Wanapum Dam museum, 98

HISTORIC BUILDINGS and SITES
Fort Vancouver National
    Monument, Vancouver, 72–73
Gaches Mansion, La Conner, 5
Willie Keil's Grave State Park,
    57–58
Lewis and Clark Interpretive
    Center, Cape Disappoint, 43
Peace Arch, Blaine, 78
Redmen Hall, Skamokawa, 62

INDIAN SITES. See NATIVE
    AMERICANS and INDIAN
    SITES
INNS and LODGING
Carson Hot Springs, 76
Chuckanut Manor Restaurant,
    Bow, 7

INNS and LOGDING (*cont.*)
Klaloch Lodge, Quinault, 46
Lake Quinault Lodge, Quinault, 46
Mio Amore Pensione, Trout Lake, 69
Oyster Creek Inn, Bow, 7
Skamania Lodge, Skamania, 76
IN the AREA
Bellingham, 7
Bickleton, 83
Columbia Gorge Route, 79
Columbia to the Sea, 64
Crab Creek Valley, 100
Gifford Pinchot Excursion, 71
Hood Canal, 39
Lewis County, 58
Mountain Loop Highway, 18
Okanogan Loop, 34
The Palouse, 94
Puget Sound to the Pend Oreille, 28–29
Snake River Canyon, 88
State 9 to Canada, 13
US 101, 51
ISLANDS
Camano Island, 3
Fidalgo Island, 4
Puget Island, 61–62
Samish Island, 6
Whidbey Island, 21–22

LAKES. See CREEKS, FALLS, LAKES, RIVERS and SPRINGS
LOCKS. See BRIDGES, DAMS, FERRIES and LOCKS
LODGING. See INNS and LODGING

MILLS, MINES and WINERIES
Columbia Crest Winery, Plymouth, 79
Monte Cristo mines, 16–17
Mont Elise Winery, Bingen, 76

Pendleton Woolen Mills, Washougal, 74
Republic mines, 27
MINES. See MILLS, MINES and WINERIES
MOUNTAINS, PASSES and VOLCANOES
Mount Adams, 68–69
Mount Baker, 11
Burley Mountain, 66–68
Chuckanut Mountain, 6–7
Deception Pass, 22
Glacier Peak, 18
Harts Pass, 24
Rainy Pass, 24
Saddle Mountain, 98–99
Sherman Creek Pass, 26, 27
Mount St. Helens, 11, 65–68
Mount Vernon, 4, 11
Washington Pass, 24
MUSEUMS. See GALLERIES, MUSEUMS, SCHOOLS and THEATERS

NATIVE AMERICANS and INDIAN SITES
Dewatto, 38
Kamiak Butte, 92
Moses Coulee, 103
Palouse, 89
Quillayute Indian Reservation, 48
Quinault Indian Reservation, 45
Skamokawa, 62
Steptoe Butte, 93, 94
Tulalip Indian Reservation, 2

OUTDOOR RECREATION
Big Four Inn, Silverton, 17
Columbia River Gorge, 76–78
Henry M. Jackson Wilderness, Darrington, 18
Kayak Point County Park, Tulalip, 2
Lake Osoyoos, Oroville, 32

Index

Larrabee State Park, Fairhaven, 7
Marymeer Falls, 49
Milwaukee Railroad track, 99
Mount Adams Wilderness
    Area, 68
Olympic National Park, 46–47,
    49, 50
Pacific Crest Trail, 24
Pyramid Peak, 49
Red Bridge Forest Service
    campground, Bear Lake, 17
Rialto Beach, La Push, 49
Sun Mountain Lodge,
    Winthrop, 25
Tiger, 28
Willapa Bay, 43–45

PARKS. See FORESTS, PARKS
    and WILDLIFE
PASSES. See MOUNTAINS,
    PASSES and VOLCANOES

RAILROADS and ROADSIDE
    SIGNS
Burma-Shave signs, 53–55
Great Northern Railroad, 17, 27
Incline Railway, Marblemount,
    23
Milwaukee Railroad, 99
RESTAURANTS
Chuckanut Manor Restaurant,
    Bow, 7
Gibson Girls Stockyard Cafe,
    Omak, 26
Mio Amore Pensione, Trout
    Lake, 69
Rhododendron Cafe, Bow, 6
Wauconda Restaurant,
    Wauconda, 27
RIVERS. See CREEKS, FALLS,
    LAKES, RIVERS and
    SPRINGS
ROADSIDE SIGNS. See
    RAILROADS and ROADSIDE
    SIGNS

SCHOOLS. See GALLERIES,
    MUSEUMS, SCHOOLS and
    THEATERS
SHIP ROCKS. See CAVES,
    COULEES, FOSSILS and
    SHIP ROCKS
SHOPS
Columbia Crest Winery,
    Plymouth, 79
North Cascades National Park,
    Sedro Woolley, 11, 22
Pendleton Woolen Mills,
    Washougal, 74
SPRINGS. See CREEKS, FALLS,
    LAKES, RIVERS and
    SPRINGS

THEATERS. See GALLERIES,
    MUSEUMS, SCHOOLS and
    THEATERS
TOURISM and TRAVEL
Chuckanut Drive, 6–7
Mountain Loop Highway,
    14–18
Seattle City Light Skagit Tours,
    23
TOWNS. See CITIES and TOWNS

VOLCANOES. See MOUNTAINS,
    PASSES and VOLCANOES

WAR SITES
Fort Casey State Park,
    Keystone, 21–22
Fort Columbia, 41
WELL-KNOWN PEOPLE
Ulysses S. Grant, 60–61
Sam Hill, 78–79
William Keil, 57–58
Lewis and Clark, 43, 85
WILDLIFE. See FORESTS, PARKS
    and WILDLIFE
WINERIES. See MILLS, MINES
    and WINERIES

Other titles in the Country Roads series:

Country Roads of Michigan
Country Roads of Massachusetts
Country Roads of Illinois
Country Roads of New Hampshire
Country Roads of Oregon
Country Roads of New York
Country Roads of Indiana
Country Roads of Ohio
Country Roads of Vermont
Country Roads of Hawaii
Country Roads of Quebec
Country Days in New York City
Country Roads of Kentucky
Country Roads of Pennsylvania

All books are $9.95 at bookstores.
Or order directly from the publisher (add $3.00
shipping & handling for direct orders):

Country Roads Press
P.O. Box 286
Castine, Maine 04421
Toll-free phone number: **800-729-9179**